LOVE AND LIVING

BOOKS BY THOMAS MERTON

The Asian Journal
Bread in the Wilderness
Conjectures of a Guilty Bystander
Contemplation in a World of Action
Disputed Questions
Gandhi on Non-Violence
Ishi Means Man
Life and Holiness
The Living Bread
Love and Living
The Monastic Journey
My Argument with the Gestapo
Mystics and Zen Masters
The New Man
New Seeds of Contemplation
No Man Is an Island
Seasons of Celebration
The Secular Journal of Thomas Merton
Seeds of Destruction
The Seven Storey Mountain
The Sign of Jonas
The Silent Life
Thoughts in Solitude
The Waters of Siloe
Zen and the Birds of Appetite

POETRY

The Collected Poems of Thomas Merton
Emblems of a Season of Fury
The Strange Islands
Selected Poems
The Tears of the Blind Lions

TRANSLATIONS

Clement of Alexandria
The Way of Chuang Tzu
The Wisdom of the Desert

THOMAS MERTON

Love and Living

EDITED BY
NAOMI BURTON STONE
&
BROTHER PATRICK HART

FARRAR · STRAUS · GIROUX
NEW YORK

LIBRARY OF CONGRESS CATALOGING IN PUBLICATION DATA

MERTON, THOMAS, 1915–1968.

LOVE AND LIVING.

1. SPIRITUAL LIFE—CATHOLIC AUTHORS—ADDRESSES, ESSAYS,

LECTURES. I. STONE, NAOMI BURTON. II. HART, PATRICK,

BROTHER. III. TITLE.

BX1751.2.M47 1979   230'.2   79–14717

Contents

III. CHRISTIAN HUMANISM

ACKNOWLEDGMENTS

Grateful acknowledgment is made to the editors and publishers of the following journals, in which some of these essays first appeared, although in considerably different form: *America, The Baptist Student, The Bible Today, Cistercian Studies, Commonweal, The Cord, The Critic, The Mediaator,* and *Spiritual Life.* "Learning to Live" was first published as a chapter in *University on the Heights,* edited by Wesley First (Doubleday, 1969), and "Symbolism: Communication or Communion?" was included in *New Directions Annual 20* (1968). Two of the "Seven Words" in part two of this volume first appeared in *Prophetic Voices,* edited by Ned O'Gorman, and published by Random House (1969). They are all reprinted here with permission of the publishers. "Christian Humanism in the Nuclear Age," although unpublished in the United States, was originally published in *Redeeming the Times* (the title under which *Seeds of Destruction* appeared in England).

I
LOVE AND LIVING

Learning to Live

Life consists in learning to live on one's own, spontaneous, freewheeling: to do this one must recognize what is one's own—be familiar and at home with oneself. This means basically learning who one is, and learning what one has to offer to the contemporary world, and then learning how to make that offering valid.

The purpose of education is to show a person how to define himself authentically and spontaneously in relation to his world—not to impose a prefabricated definition of the world, still less an arbitrary definition of the individual himself. The world is made up of the people who are fully alive in it: that is, of the people who can be themselves in it and can enter into a living and fruitful relationship with each other in it. The world is, therefore, more real in proportion as the people in it are able to be more fully and more humanly alive: that is to say, better able to make a lucid and conscious use of their freedom. Basically, this freedom must consist first of all in the capacity to choose their own lives, to find themselves on the deepest possible level. A superficial freedom to wander aimlessly here or there, to taste this or that, to make a choice of distractions (in Pascal's sense) is simply a sham. It claims to be a freedom of "choice" when it has evaded the basic task of discovering who it is that chooses. It is not free because it is unwilling to face the risk of self-discovery.

The function of a university is, then, first of all to help the student to discover himself: to recognize himself, and to identify who it is that chooses.

This description will be recognized at once as unconventional and, in fact, monastic. To put it in even more outrageous terms, the function of the university is to help men and women save their souls and, in so doing, to save their society: from what? From the hell of meaninglessness, of obsession, of complex artifice, of systematic lying, of criminal evasions and neglects, of self-destructive futilities.

It will be evident from my context that the business of saving one's soul means more than taking an imaginary object, "a soul," and entrusting it to some institutional bank for deposit until it is recovered with interest in heaven.

Speaking as a Christian existentialist, I mean by "soul" not simply the Aristotelian essential form but the mature personal identity, the creative fruit of an authentic and lucid search, the "self" that is found after other partial and exterior selves have been discarded as masks.

This metaphor must not mislead: this inner identity is not "found" as an object, but is the very self that finds. It is lost when it forgets to find, when it does not know how to seek, or when it seeks itself as an object. (Such a search is futile and self-contradictory.) Hence the paradox that it finds best when it stops seeking: and the graduate level of learning is when one learns to sit still and be what one has become, which is what one does not know and does not need to know. In the language of Sufism, the end of the ascetic life is *Rida,* satisfaction. Debts are paid (and they were largely imaginary). One no longer seeks something else. One no longer seeks to be told by another who one is. One no longer demands reassurance. But there is the whole infinite depth of *what is* remaining to be revealed. And it is not revealed to those who seek it from others.

Education in this sense means more than learning; and for such education, one is awarded no degree. One graduates by rising from the dead. Learning to be oneself means, therefore, learning to die in order to live. It means discovering in the ground of one's being a "self" which is ultimate and indestructible, which not only survives the destruction of all other more superficial selves but finds its identity affirmed and clarified by their destruction.

The inmost self is naked. Nakedness is not socially acceptable except in certain crude forms which can be commercialized without any effort of imagination (topless waitresses). Curiously, this cult of bodily nakedness is a veil and a distraction, a communion in futility, where all identities get lost in their nerve endings. Everybody claims to like it. Yet no one is really happy with it. It makes money.

Spiritual nakedness, on the other hand, is far too stark to be useful. It strips life down to the root where life and death are equal, and this is what nobody likes to look at. But it is where freedom really begins: the freedom that cannot be guaranteed by the death of somebody else. The point where you become free not to kill, not to exploit, not to destroy, not to compete, because you are no longer afraid of death or the devil or poverty or failure. If you discover this nakedness, you'd better keep it private. People don't like it. But can you keep it private? Once you are exposed . . . Society continues to do you the service of keeping you in disguises, not for your comfort, but for its own. It is quite willing to strip you of this or that outer skin (a stripping which is a normal ritual and which everybody enjoys). The final metaphysical stripping goes too far, unless you happen to be in Auschwitz.

If I say this description is "monastic," I do not necessarily mean "theological." The terms in which it has been stated here are open to interpretation on several levels: theologically, ascetically, liturgically, psychologically. Let's assume that this last is the more acceptable level for most readers. And let's assume that I am simply speaking from experience as one who, from a French lycée and an English public school, has traveled through various places of "learning" and has, in these, learned one thing above all: to keep on going. I have described the itinerary elsewhere,* but perhaps a few new ideas may be added here. The journey went from Europe to America, from Cambridge to Columbia. At Columbia, having got the necessary degrees, I crossed the boundary that separates those who learn as students from those who learn as teachers. Then I went to teach English at a Catholic college (St. Bonaventure).† After which I went to be a novice in a Trappist monastery, where I also "learned" just enough theology to renounce all desire to be a theologian. Here also (for I am still in Kentucky) I learned by teaching: not theology as such, but the more hazardous and less charted business of monastic education, which deals with the whole person in a situation of considerable ambiguity and hazard: the novice, the young monk who wants to become a contemplative and who is (you sooner or later discover) trapped both by the institution and by his own character in a situation where what he desperately wants beyond all else on earth will probably turn out to be impossible. Perhaps I would have been safer back at Columbia teaching elementary English composition. Fortunately, I am no longer teaching anybody anything.

On the basis of this experience, I can, anyhow, take up an ancient position that views monastery and university as having

* See Thomas Merton's autobiography, *The Seven Storey Mountain* (Octagon Books), for a more complete account of his youthful itinerary. —Ed.

† Now St. Bonaventure University.

the same kind of function. After all, that is natural enough to one who could walk about Cambridge saying to himself, "Here were the Franciscans at one time, here the Dominicans, here—at my own college—Chaucer was perhaps a clerk."

A university, like a monastery (and here I have medievalists to back me up, but presume that footnotes are not needed), is at once a microcosm and a paradise. Both monastery and university came into being in a civilization open to the sacred, that is to say, in a civilization which paid a great deal of attention to what it considered to be its own primordial roots in a mythical and archetypal holy ground, a spiritual creation. Thus the *Logos* or *Ratio* of both monastery and university is pretty much the same. Both are "schools," and they teach not so much by imparting information as by bringing the clerk (in the university) or the monk (in the monastery) to direct contact with "the beginning," the archetypal paradise world. This was often stated symbolically by treating the various disciplines of university and monastic life, respectively, as the "four rivers of paradise." At the same time, university and monastery tended sometimes to be in very heated conflict, for though they both aimed at "participation" in and "experience" of the hidden and sacred values implanted in the "ground" and the "beginning," they arrived there by different means: the university by *scientia,* intellectual knowledge, and the monastery by *sapientia,* or mystical contemplation. (Of course, the monastery itself easily tended to concentrate on *scientia*—the science of the Scriptures—and in the university there could be mystics like Aquinas, Scotus, and Eckhart. So that in the end, in spite of all the fulminations of the Cistercian St. Bernard, a deeper *sapientia* came sometimes from schools than from monasteries.)

The point I am making here is this: far from suggesting that Columbia ought to return to the ideal of Chartres and concentrate on the trivium and quadrivium, I am insinuating that this archetypal approach, this "microcosm-paradise" type of sacred humanism, is basically personalistic.

I admit that all through the Middle Ages men were actively curious about the exact location of the earthly paradise. This curiosity was not absent from the mind of Columbus. The Pilgrim Fathers purified it a little, spiritualized it a little, but New England to them was a kind of paradise: and to make sure of a paradisic institution they created, of all things, Harvard. But the monks of the Middle Ages, and the clerks too, believed that the inner paradise was the ultimate ground of freedom in man's heart. To find it one had to travel, as Augustine had said, not with steps, but with yearnings. The journey was from man's "fallen" condition, in which he was not free not to be untrue to himself, to that original freedom in which, made in the image and likeness of God, he was no longer able to be untrue to himself. Hence, he recovered that nakedness of Adam which needed no fig leaves of law, of explanation, of justification, and no social garments of skins (Gregory of Nyssa). Paradise is simply the person, the self, but the radical self in its uninhibited freedom. The self no longer clothed with an ego.

One must not forget the dimension of relatedness to others. True freedom is openness, availability, the capacity for gift. But we must also remember that the difficult dialectic of fidelity to others in fidelity to oneself requires one to break through the veils of infidelity which, as individual egoists or as a selfish community, we set up to prevent ourselves from living in the truth.

This sacred humanism was, of course, abused and perverted by the sacred institution, and in the end monasticism, by a curious reversal that is so usual in the evolution of societies, identified the fig leaf with the paradise condition and insisted on the monk having at least enough of a self to serve the organization—itself pressed into the service of more mundane interests. Freedom, then, consisted in blind obedience, and contemplation consisted in renouncing nakedness in favor of elaborate and ritual vestments. The "person" was only what he was in the eyes of the institution because the institution was, for all intents and purposes, Paradise, the domain of God, and indeed God himself. To be in Paradise, then, consisted in being defined by the paradisic community—or by Academe. Hence, the dogmatic absolutism for which the late Middle Ages are all too well known—and for which they are by no means uniquely responsible.

The original and authentic "paradise" idea, both in the monastery (*paradisus claustralis*) and in the university, implied not simply a celestial store of theoretic ideas to which the Magistri and Doctores held the key, but the inner self of the student who, in discovering the ground of his own personality as it opened out into the center of all created being, found in himself the light and the wisdom of his Creator, a light and wisdom in which everything comprehensible could be comprehended and what was not comprehensible could nevertheless be grasped in the darkness of contemplation by a direct and existential contact.

Thus, the fruit of education, whether in the university (as for Eckhart) or in the monastery (as for Ruysbroeck) was the activation of that inmost center, that *scintilla animae,* that "apex" or "spark" which is a freedom beyond freedom, an identity beyond essence, a self beyond all ego, a being beyond the created realm, and a consciousness that transcends all division, all separation. To activate this spark is not to be, like Plotinus, "alone with the Alone," but to recognize the Alone which is by itself in everything because there is nothing that can be apart from It and yet nothing that can be with It, and nothing that can realize It. It can only realize itself. The "spark" which is my true self is the flash of the Absolute recognizing itself in me.

This realization at the apex is a coincidence of all opposites (as Nicholas of Cusa might say), a fusion of freedom and unfreedom, being and unbeing, life and death, self and non-self, man and God. The "spark" is not so much a stable entity which one finds but an event, an explosion which happens as all opposites clash within oneself. Then it is seen that the ego is not. It vanishes in its non-seeing when the flash of the spark alone is. When all things are reduced to the spark, who sees it? Who knows it? If you say "God," you are destroyed; and if you say no one, you will plunge into hell; and if you say I, you prove you are not even in the ballgame.

The purpose of all learning is to dispose man for this kind of event.

The purpose of various disciplines is to provide ways or paths which lead to this capacity for ignition.

Obviously it would be a grave mistake to do, as some have done and still do, and declare that the only way is to be found in a cloister and the only discipline is asceticism or Zen sitting or, for that matter, turning on with a new drug. The whole of life is learning to ignite without dependence on any specific external means, whether cloistered, Zenist Tantric, psychedelic, or what have you. It is learning that the spark, being a flash at the apex and explosion of all freedoms, can never be subject to control or to enlightenment, can never be got by pressing buttons. A spark that goes off when you swallow something or stick yourself with something may be a fairly passable imitation of the real thing, but it is not the real thing. (I will not argue that it cannot teach you a great deal about the real thing.) In the same way a cloistered complacency—a "peace" that is guaranteed only by getting out of the traffic, turning off the radio, and forgetting the world—is not by itself the real thing either.

The danger of education, I have found, is that it so easily confuses means with ends. Worse than that, it quite easily forgets both and devotes itself merely to the mass production of uneducated graduates—people literally unfit for anything except to take part in an elaborate and completely artificial charade which they and their contemporaries have conspired to call "life."

A few years ago a man who was compiling a book entitled *Success* wrote and asked me to contribute a statement on how I got to be a success. I replied indignantly that I was not able to consider myself a success in any terms that had a meaning to me. I swore I had spent my life strenuously avoiding success. If it so happened that I had once written a best seller, this was a pure accident, due to inattention and naïveté, and I would take very good care never to do the same again. If I had a message to my contemporaries, I said, it was surely this: Be anything you like, be madmen, drunks, and bastards of every shape and form, but at all costs avoid one thing: success. I heard no more from him and I am not aware that my reply was published with the other testimonials.

Thus, I have undercut all hope of claiming that Columbia made me a success. On the contrary, I believe I can thank Columbia, among so many other things, for having helped me learn the value of unsuccess. Columbia was for me a microcosm, a little world, where I exhausted myself in time. Had I waited until after graduation, it would have been too late. During the few years in which I was there, I managed to do so many wrong things that I was ready to blow my mind. But fortunately I learned, in so doing, that this was good. I might have ended up on Madison Avenue if I hadn't. Instead of preparing me for one of those splendid jobs, Columbia cured me forever of wanting one. Instead of adapting me to the world downtown, Columbia did me the favor of lobbing me half conscious into the Village, where I occasionally came to my senses and where I continued to learn. I think I have sufficiently explained, elsewhere,* how much I owed, in this regard, to people like Mark Van Doren (who lived around the corner from me in the Village) and Joseph Wood Krutch (who became, as I have become, a hermit). Such people taught me to imitate not Rockefeller but Thoreau. Of course, I am not trying to say that one has to be Thoreau rather than Rockefeller, nor am I slyly intimating that I have discovered a superior form of resentment, an offbeat way of scoring on everybody by refusing to keep score.

What I am saying is this: the score is not what matters. Life does not have to be regarded as a game in which scores are kept and somebody wins. If you are too intent on winning, you will never enjoy playing. If you are too obsessed with success, you will forget to live. If you have learned only how to be a success, your life has probably been wasted. If a university concentrates on producing successful people, it is lamentably failing in its obligation to society and to the students themselves.

Now I know that even in the thirties, at Columbia, the business of wanting to be a success was very much in the air. There was, in fact, a scandal about the yearbook senior poll. The man who was voted "most likely to succeed" was accused of having doctored the results in his own favor after a surreptitious deal with a yearbook staff member who was voted "best dressed." Incidentally, I was voted best writer. I was

---

* For further information on the Columbia days, especially the enormous influence of Mark Van Doren, see *The Seven Storey Mountain*.

not accused of trickery, but everyone understood that the vote, which had been between me and Hank Liebermann, had been decided by my fraternity brothers. (Incidentally, whatever became of the man "most likely to succeed"?)

In any case, no one really cared. Since that time many of my classmates have attained to eminence with all its joys and all its sorrows, and the ones I have seen since then are marked by the signature of anguish. So am I. I do not claim exemption. Yet I never had the feeling that our alma mater just wanted us to become well-paid operators, or to break our necks to keep on the front pages of the *Times*. On the contrary—maybe this is a delusion, but if it is a delusion it is a salutary one—I always felt at Columbia that people around me, half amused and perhaps at times half incredulous, were happy to let me be myself. (I add that I seldom felt this way at Cambridge.) The thing I always liked best about Columbia was the sense that the university was on the whole glad to turn me loose in its library, its classrooms, and among its distinguished faculty, and let me make what I liked out of it all. I did. And I ended up by being turned on like a pinball machine by Blake, Thomas Aquinas, Augustine, Eckhart, Coomaraswamy, Traherne, Hopkins, Maritain, and the sacraments of the Catholic Church. After which I came to the monastery in which (this is public knowledge) I have continued to be the same kind of maverick and have, in fact, ended as a hermit who is also fully identified with the peace movement, with Zen, with a group of Latin American hippie poets, etc., etc.

The least of the work of learning is done in classrooms. I can remember scores of incidents, remarks, happenings, encounters that took place all over the campus and sometimes far from the campus: small bursts of light that pointed out my way in the dark of my own identity. For instance, Mark Van Doren saying to me as we crossed Amsterdam Avenue:

"Well, if you have a vocation to the monastic life, it will not be possible for you to decide not to enter" (or words to that effect). I grasped at once the existential truth of this statement.

One other scene, much later on. A room in Butler Hall, overlooking some campus buildings. Daisetz Suzuki, with his great bushy eyebrows and the hearing aid that aids nothing. Mihoko, his beautiful secretary, has to repeat everything. She is making tea. Tea ceremony, but a most unconventional one, for there are no rites and no rules. I drink my tea as reverently and attentively as I can. She goes into the other room. Suzuki, as if waiting for her to go, hastily picks up his cup and drains it.

It was at once as if nothing at all had happened and as if the roof had flown off the building. But in reality nothing had happened. A very very old deaf Zen man with bushy eyebrows had drunk a cup of tea, as though with the complete wakefulness of a child and as though at the same time declaring with utter finality: "This is not important!"

The function of a university is to teach a man how to drink tea, not because anything is important, but because it is usual to drink tea, or, for that matter, anything else under the sun. And whatever you do, every act, however small, can teach you everything—provided you see who it is that is acting.

Love and Solitude

AUTHOR'S NOTE: The following pages were originally written as a preface for the Japanese translation of *Thoughts in Solitude*. They are here revised to form an essay on the solitary life, on contemplation, and on basic monastic values which are today called into question even by monks themselves. The purpose of these notes is not to elaborate a defense of solitude—which is often condemned or defended without having been understood—but simply to let solitude speak a little and say something for itself. In the original preface, I felt that many Japanese readers, still open to their more contemplative heritage, would recognize something familiar to them in these intuitive, provisional, and deliberately incomplete suggestions. It is possible that Western readers will simply dismiss them with impatience.

No writing on the solitary, meditative dimensions of life can say anything that has not already been said better by the wind in the pine trees. These pages seek nothing more than to echo the silence and the peace that is "heard" when the rain wanders freely among the hills and forests. But what can the wind say where there is no hearer? There is then a deeper silence: the silence in which the Hearer is No-Hearer. That deeper silence must be heard before one can speak truly of solitude.

These pages do not attempt to convey any special information, or to answer deep philosophical questions about life. True, they do concern themselves with questions about life.

But they certainly do not pretend to do the reader's thinking for him. On the contrary, they invite him to listen for himself. They do not merely speak to him, they remind him that he is a Hearer.

But who is this Hearer?

Beyond the Hearer, is there perhaps No-Hearer?

Who is this No-Hearer?

For such outrageous questions there are no intelligible answers. The only answer is the Hearing itself. The proper climate for such Hearing is solitude.

Or perhaps better, this Hearing which is No-Hearing is itself solitude. Why do I speak of a Hearing which is No-Hearing? Because if you imagine the solitary as "one" who has numerically isolated himself from "many others," who has simply gone out of the crowd to hang up his individual number on a rock in the desert, and there to receive messages denied to the many, you have a false and demonic solitude. This is solipsism, not solitude. It is the false unity of separateness, in which the individual marks himself off as his own number, affirms himself by saying "count me out."

The true unity of the solitary life is the one in which there is no possible division. The true solitary does not seek himself, but loses himself. He forgets that there is number in order to become all. Therefore, he is No (individual) Hearer.

He is attuned to all the Hearing in the world, since he lives in silence. He does not listen to the ground of being, but he identifies himself with that ground in which all being hears and knows itself. Therefore, he no longer has a thought for himself. What is this ground, this unity? It is Love. The paradox of solitude is that its true ground is universal love— and true solitude is the undivided unity of love for which there is no number.

The world is shrinking. There is less and less space in which men can be alone. It is said that if we go on increasing at our present rate, in six hundred and fifty years there will be only one square foot left for every person. Even then (someone may say) there will be one square foot of solitude. But is that right? Is each person a separate solitude of his own? No. There is One Solitude in which all persons are at once together and alone. But the price of a mathematical, quantitative concept of man (for instance in a positivistic and sociological approach) is that in reducing each individual to his own number it reduces him to nothing: and in making the mass of men simply a total of individual units, it makes of it an enormous statistical void—in which numbers simply proliferate without aim, without value, without meaning, without love.

The peril of this massive, numerical, technical concept of man is, then, that it destroys love by substituting the individual for the person. And what is the person? Precisely, he is one in the unity which is love. He is undivided in himself because he is open to all. He is open to all because the one love that is the source of all, the form of all, and the end of all is one in him and in all. He is truly alone who is wide open to heaven and earth and closed to no one.

Love is not a problem, not an answer to a question. Love knows no question. It is the ground of all, and questions arise only insofar as we are divided, absent, estranged, alienated from that ground.

But the precise nature of our society is to bring about this division, this alienation, this estrangement, this absence. Hence, we live in a world in which, though we clutter it with our possessions, our projects, our exploitations, and our machinery, we ourselves are absent. Hence, we live in a world in which we say, "God is dead," and do so in a sense rightly, since we are no longer capable of experiencing the truth that we are completely rooted and grounded in His Love.

How can we rediscover this truth?

Only when we no longer need to seek it—for as long as we seek it we imply that we have lost it. But, in fact, to recognize ourselves as grounded in our true ground, love, is to recognize that we cannot be without it.

This recognition is impossible without a basic personal solitude.

Collective agitation, no matter how much it expostulates about "I and Thou," will never attain it. For, in the ground of solitude, "I and Thou" are one. And only from this ground does true dilection grow. Let us not then make "love" and "solitude" a matter of question and answer. The answer is not found in words, but by living on a certain level of consciousness. These pages are, then, concerned with a spiritual climate, an atmosphere, a landscape of the mind, a level of consciousness: the peace, the silence of aloneness in which the Hearer listens, and the Hearing is No-Hearing.

Christianity is a religion of the Word. The Word is Love. But we sometimes forget that the Word emerges first of all from silence. When there is no silence, then the One Word which God speaks is not truly heard as Love. Then only "words" are heard. "Words" are not love, for they are many and Love is One. Where there are many words, we lose consciousness of the fact that there is really only One Word. The One Word which God speaks is Himself. Speaking, He manifests Himself as infinite Love. His speaking and His hearing are One. So silent is His speech that, to our way of thinking, His speech is no-speech, His hearing is no-hearing. Yet in his silence, in the abyss of His one Love, all words are spoken and all words are heard. Only in this silence of infinite Love do they have coherence and meaning. Yet we draw them out of silence in order to separate them from one another, to make them distinct, to give them a unique sound by which we can discern them. This is necessary. Yet in all these many sounds and concepts there remains the hidden, secret power of one silence, one love, which is the power of God. "When all things were enveloped in quiet silence," says the Book of Wisdom (18:14), "and when the night had reached the mid-point in its course, from the height of the heavens Thy all powerful Word leaped down from the royal throne." By the action that takes place in life and history the secret non-action of Word and power manifest their reality. In this deep silence, Love remains the ground of history.

Even though one may be a learned man and may have profound knowledge of many subjects, and many "words," this is of no value, it has no central meaning, . . . if the One Word, Love, has not been heard. That One Word is heard only in the silence and solitude of the empty heart, the selfless, undivided heart, the heart that is at peace, detached, free, without care. In the language of Christianity, this freedom is the realm of faith, and hope, but above all of Love. "If I have perfect faith . . . but no Love, I am nothing" (I Corinthians 13:2). "Anyone who does not Love is still in death" (I John 3:14).

When the Christian faith is made to appear very complicated, it seems to consist of numerous doctrines, a complex system of concepts which impart information about the supernatural and seems to answer all possible questions about the afterlife, and about the means to attain to happiness in heaven. While these doctrines may be very true, they cannot be understood if we think that the only purpose of faith is multiple information communicated in many complex doctrines. In fact, the object of faith is One—God, Love. And though the revealed doctrines about Him are true, yet what they tell us of Him is not fully adequate as long as we grasp them only separately, incoherently, without living unity in Love. They must converge upon Love as the spokes of a wheel converge

upon a central hub. They are window frames through which
the One Light enters our houses. The window frame is precise and distinct: yet what we really see is the light itself,
which is diffuse and all-pervading, so that it is everywhere
and nowhere. No mind can comprehend God's reality, as it
is in itself, and if we approach Him we must advance not only
by knowing but by not-knowing. We must seek to communicate with Him, not only by words, but above all by silence,
in which there is only the One Word, and the One Word is
infinite Love and endless silence.

Where is silence? Where is solitude? Where is Love?
Ultimately, these cannot be found anywhere except in the
ground of our own being. There, in the silent depths, there
is no more distinction between the I and the Not-I. There is
perfect peace, because we are grounded in infinite creative and
redemptive Love. There we encounter God, whom no eye can
see, and in Whom, as St. Paul says, "we live and move and
have our being" (Acts 17:28). In Him, too, we find solitude,
as St. John of the Cross said, we find that the All and the
Nothing encounter one another and are the Same.

If there is no silence beyond and within the many words
of doctrine, there is no religion, only a religious ideology. For
religion goes beyond words and actions, and attains to the
ultimate truth only in silence and Love. Where this silence
is lacking, where there are only the "many words" and not
the One Word, then there is much bustle and activity but no
peace, no deep thought, no understanding, no inner quiet.
Where there is no peace, there is no light and no Love. The
mind that is hyperactive seems to itself to be awake and productive, but it is dreaming, driven by fantasy and doubt.
Only in silence and solitude, in the quiet of worship, the rev-
erent peace of prayer, the adoration in which the entire ego-

self silences and abases itself in the presence of the Invisible
God to receive His one Word of Love; only in these "activities" which are "non-actions" does the spirit truly wake from
the dream of a multifarious, confused, and agitated existence.

Precisely because of this, modern Western man is afraid
of solitude. He is unable to be alone, to be silent. He is communicating his spiritual and mental sickness to men of the
East. Asia is gravely tempted by the violence and activism of
the West, and is gradually losing hold of its traditional respect
for silent wisdom. Therefore, it is all the more necessary, at
this time, to rediscover the climate of solitude and of silence:
not that everyone can go apart and live alone. But in moments
of silence, of meditation, of enlightenment and peace, one
learns to be silent and alone everywhere. One learns to live
in the atmosphere of solitude even in the midst of crowds.
Not "divided," but one with all in God's Love. For one
learns to be a Hearer who is No-Hearer, and one learns to
forget all words and listen only to the One Word which seems
to be No-Word. One opens the inner door of his heart to the
infinite silences of the Spirit, out of whose abysses love wells
up without fail and gives itself to all. In His silence, the meaning of every sound is finally clear. Only in His silence can the
truth of words be distinguished, not in their separateness, but
in their pointing to the central unity of Love. All words,
then, say one thing only: that *all is Love*.

Heidegger has said that our relation to what is closest to us
is always confused and without vigor. What is closer to us
than the solitude which is the ground of our being? It is
always there. For that precise reason it is always ignored, for
when we begin to think of it we are uncomfortable, we make
an "object" of it, and our relation to it is falsified. And truly,
we are so close to ourselves that there is really no "relation"

to the ground of our own being. Can we not simply *be* ourselves without thinking about it? This is true solitude.

Is it true to say that one goes into solitude to "get at the root of existence"? It would be better simply to say that in solitude one *is* at the root. He who is alone, and is conscious of what his solitude means, finds himself simply in the ground of life. He is "in Love." He is in love with all, with everyone, with everything. He is not surprised at this, and he is able to live with this disconcerting and unexciting reality, which has no explanation. He lives, then, as a seed planted in the ground. As Christ said, the seed in the ground must die. To be as a seed in the ground of one's very life is to dissolve in that ground in order to become fruitful. One disappears into Love, in order to "be Love." But this fruitfulness is beyond any planning and any understanding of man. To be "fruitful" in this sense, one must forget every idea of fruitfulness or productivity, and merely *be*. One's fruitfulness is at once an act of faith and an act of doubt: doubt of all that one has hitherto seen in oneself, and faith in what one cannot possibly imagine for oneself. The "doubt" dissolves our ego-identity. Faith gives us life in Christ, according to St. Paul's word: "I live, now not I, but Christ lives in me" (Galatians 2:20). To accept this is impossible unless one has profound hope in the incomprehensible fruitfulness that emerges from this dissolution of our ego in the ground of being and of Love. Such a hope is not the product of human reason, it is a secret gift of grace. It sustains us with divine and hidden aid. To accept our own dissolution would be inhuman if we did not at the same time accept the wholeness and completeness of everything in God's Love. We accept our emptying because we realize that our very emptiness is fulfillment and plenitude. In our emptiness the One Word is clearly spoken. It says, "I will never let go of you or desert you" (Hebrews 13:5), for I am your God, I am Love.

To leave this ground in order to plunge into the human and social process with multiple activities may well be only illusion, a purely imaginary fruitfulness.

Modern man believes he is fruitful and productive when his ego is aggressively affirmed, when he is visibly active, and when his action produces obvious results. But this activity is more and more filled with self-contradiction. The richest and most scientific culture in the world, potentially organized for unlimited production, is expending its huge force and wealth, not on fruitfulness, but on instruments of destruction. In such condition, even though men sincerely desire peace, their desire is only an illusion which cannot find fulfillment. Such men live in perpetual self-defeat.

To rebel against this self-defeat by a morbid self-imprisonment in the disillusioned ego would be a merely false solitude. Solitude is not withdrawal from ordinary life. It is not apart from, above, "better than" ordinary life; on the contrary, solitude is the very ground of ordinary life. It is the very ground of that simple, unpretentious, fully human activity by which we quietly earn our daily living and share our experiences with a few intimate friends. But we must learn to know and accept this ground of our being. To most people, though it is always there, it is unthinkable and unknown. Consequently, their life has no center and no foundation. It is dispersed in a pretense of "togetherness" in which there is no real meaning. Only when our activity proceeds out of the ground in which we have consented to be dissolved does it have the divine fruitfulness of love and grace. Only then does it really reach others in true communion. Often our need for others is not love at all but only the need to be sustained in our illusions, even as we sustain others in theirs. But when we have renounced these illusions, then we can certainly go out to others in true compassion. It is in solitude that illusions finally dissolve. But one must work hard to see that they do not reshape themselves in some worse form, peopling our solitude with devils disguised as angels of light. Love, simplicity, and compassion protect us against this. He who is truly alone finds in himself the heart of compassion with which to love not only this man or that but all men. He sees them all in the One who is the Word of God, the perfect manifestation of God's Love, Jesus Christ.

Love and Need: Is Love a Package or a Message?

We speak of "falling in love," as though love were something like water that collects in pools, lakes, rivers, and oceans. You can "fall into" it or walk around it. You can sail on it or swim in it, or you can just look at it from a safe distance. This expression seems to be peculiar to the English language. French, for instance, does not speak of *"tomber en amour"* but does mention "falling amorous." The Italian and Spanish say one "enamors oneself." Latins do not regard love as a passive accident. Our English expression "to fall in love" suggests an unforeseen mishap that may or may not be fatal. You are at a party: you have had more drinks than you need. You decide to walk around the garden a little. You don't notice the swimming pool . . . all at once you have to swim! Fortunately, they fish you out, and you are wet but none the worse for wear. Love is like that. If you don't look where you are going, you are liable to land in it: the experience will normally be slightly ridiculous. Your friends will all find it funny, and if they happen to be around at the time, they will do their best to steer you away from the water and into a nice comfortable chair where you can go to sleep.

Sometimes, of course, the pool is empty. Then you don't get wet, you just crack your skull or break your arm.

To speak of "falling into" something is to shift responsibility from your own will to a cosmic force like gravitation. You "fall" when you are carried off by a power beyond your control. Once you start you can't stop. You're gone. You don't know where you may land. We also speak of "falling into a coma" or "falling into disgrace," or "falling into bankruptcy." A thesaurus reminds us one can "fall into decay," "fall on the ear," and even "fall flat on the ear." A certain rudimentary theology regards the whole human race as "fallen" because Eve tempted Adam to love her. That is bad theology. Sex is not original sin. (A better view is that the love of Adam for Eve was originally meant as a communion and a diversity-in-oneness which reflected the invisible God in visible creation for "God is love.")

The expression to "fall in love" reflects a peculiar attitude toward love and toward life itself—a mixture of fear, awe, fascination, and confusion. It implies suspicion, doubt, hesitation, in the presence of something unavoidable—yet not fully reliable. For love takes you out of yourself. You lose control. You "fall." You get hurt. It upsets the ordinary routine of life. You become emotional, imaginative, vulnerable, foolish. You are no longer content to eat and sleep, make money and have fun. You now have to let yourself be carried away with this force that is stronger than reason and more imperious even than business!

Obviously, if you are a cool and self-possessed character, you will take care never to *fall*. You will accept the unavoidable power of love as a necessity that can be controlled and turned to good account. You will confine it to the narrow category of "fun" and so you will not let it get out of hand. You will have fun by making others fall without falling yourself.

But the question of love is one that cannot be evaded. Whether or not you claim to be interested in it, from the moment you are alive you are bound to be concerned with love, because love is not just something that happens to you: *it is a certain special way of being alive.*

Love is, in fact, an intensification of life, a completeness, a fullness, a wholeness of life. We do not live merely in order to vegetate through our days until we die. Nor do we live merely in order to take part in the routines of work and amusement that go on around us. We are not just machines that have to be cared for and driven carefully until they run down. In other words, life is not a straight horizontal line between two points, birth and death. Life curves upward to a peak of intensity, a high point of value and meaning, at which all its latent creative possibilities go into action and the person transcends himself or herself in encounter, response, and communion with another. It is for this that we came into the world—this communion and self-transcendence. We do not become fully human until we give ourselves to each other in love. And this must not be confined only to sexual fulfillment: it embraces everything in the human person—the capacity for self-giving, for sharing, for creativity, for mutual care, for spiritual concern.

Love is our true destiny. We do not find the meaning of life by ourselves alone—we find it with another. We do not discover the secret of our lives merely by study and calculation in our own isolated meditations. The meaning of our life is a secret that has to be revealed to us in love, *by the one we love.* And if this love is unreal, the secret will not be found, the meaning will never reveal itself, the message will never be decoded. At best, we will receive a scrambled and partial message, one that will deceive and confuse us. We will never be fully real until we let ourselves fall in love—either with another human person or with God.

Hence, our attitude toward life is also going to be in one way or another an attitude toward love. Our conception of ourselves is bound to be profoundly affected by our conception—and our experience—of love. And our love, or our lack of it, our willingness to risk it or our determination to avoid it, will in the end be an expression of ourselves: of who we think we are, of what we want to be, of what we think we are here for.

Nor will this be merely something that goes on in our head. Love affects more than our thinking and our behavior toward those we love. It transforms our entire life. Genuine love is a personal revolution. Love takes your ideas, your desires, and your actions and welds them together in one experience and one living reality which is a new *you*. You may prefer to keep this from happening. You may keep your thoughts, desires, and acts in separate compartments if you want: but then you will be an artificial and divided person, with three little filing cabinets: one of ideas, one of decisions, and one of actions and experiences. These three compartments may not have much to do with each other. Such a life does not make sense, and is not likely to be happy. The contents of the separate filing cabinets may become increasingly peculiar as life goes on. Our philosophy of life is not something we create all by ourselves out of nothing. Our ways of thinking, even our attitudes toward ourselves, are more and more determined from the outside. Even our love tends to fit into ready-made forms. We consciously or unconsciously tailor our notions of love according to the patterns that we are exposed to day after day in advertising, in movies, on TV, and in our reading. One of these prevailing ready-made attitudes toward life and love needs to be discussed here. It is one that is seldom consciously spelled out. It is just "in the air," something that one is exposed to without thinking about it. This idea of love is a corollary of the thinking that holds our marketing society together. It is what one might call a package concept of love.

Love is regarded as a deal. The deal presupposes that we all have needs which have to be fulfilled by means of exchange. In order to make a deal you have to appear in the market with a worthwhile product, or if the product is worthless, you can get by if you dress it up in a good-looking package. We unconsciously think of ourselves as objects for sale on the market. We want to be wanted. We want to attract customers. We want to look like the kind of product that makes money. Hence, we waste a great deal of time modeling ourselves on the images presented to us by an affluent marketing society.

In doing this we come to consider ourselves and others not as *persons* but as *products*—as "goods," or in other words, as packages. We appraise one another commercially. We size each other up and make deals with a view to our own profit. We do not give ourselves in love, we make a deal that will enhance our own product, and therefore no deal is final. Our eye is already on the next deal—and this next deal need not necessarily be with the same customer. Life is more interesting when you make a lot of deals with a lot of new customers.

This view, which equates lovemaking with salesmanship and love with a glamorous package, is based on the idea of love as a mechanism of instinctive needs. We are biological machines endowed with certain urges that require fulfillment. If we are smart, we can exploit and manipulate these urges in ourselves and in others. We can turn them to our own advantage. We can cash in on them, using them to satisfy and enrich our own ego by profitable deals with other egos. If the partner is not too smart, a little cheating won't hurt, especially if it makes everything more profitable and more satisfactory for me!

If this process of making deals and satisfying needs begins to speed up, life becomes an exciting gambling game. We meet more and more others with the same needs. We are all spilled out helter-skelter onto a roulette wheel hoping to land on a propitious number. This happens over and over again. "Falling in love" is a droll piece of luck that occurs when you end up with another person whose need more or less fits in with yours. You are somehow able to fulfill each other, to complete each other. You have won the sweepstake. Of course, the prize is good only for a couple of years. You have to get back in the game. But occasionally you win. Others are not so lucky. They never meet anyone with just the right kind of need to go with their need. They never find anyone with the right combination of qualities, gimmicks, and weaknesses. They never seem to buy the right package. They never land on the right number. They fall into the pool and the pool is empty.

This concept of love assumes that the machinery of buying and selling of needs and fulfillment is what makes everything run. It regards life as a market and love as a variation on free enterprise. You buy and you sell, and to get somewhere in love is to make a good deal with whatever you happen to have available. In business, buyer and seller get together in the market with their needs and their products. And they swap. The swapping is simplified by the use of a happy-making convenience called money. So too in love. The love relationship is a deal that is arrived at for the satisfaction of mutual needs. If it is successful it pays off, not necessarily in money, but in gratification, peace of mind, fulfillment. Yet since the idea of happiness is with us inseparable from the idea of prosperity, we must face the fact that a love that is not crowned with every material and social benefit seems to us to be rather suspect. Is it really *blessed?* Was it really a *deal?*

The trouble with this commercialized idea of love is that it diverts your attention more and more from the essentials to the accessories of love. You are no longer able to really love the other person, for you become obsessed with the effectiveness of your own package, your own product, your own market value.

At the same time, the transaction itself assumes an exaggerated importance. For many people what matters is the delightful and fleeting moment in which the deal is closed. They give little thought to what the deal itself represents. That is perhaps why so many marriages do not last, and why so many people have to remarry. They cannot feel real if they just make one contract and leave it at that!

In the past, in a society where people lived on the land, where the possession of land represented the permanence and security of one's family, there was no problem about marriage for life: it was perfectly natural and it was accepted without even unconscious resistance. Today, one's security and one's identity have to be constantly reaffirmed: nothing is permanent, everything is in movement. You have to move with it. You have to come up with something new each day. Every morning you have to prove that you are still there. You have to keep making deals.

Each deal needs to have the freshness, the uniqueness, the paradisal innocence of closing with a brand-new customer. Whether we like it or not, we are dominated by an "ethic," or perhaps better, a "superstition" of quantity. We do not believe in a single lasting value that is established once for all —a permanent and essential quality that is never obsolete or stale. We are obsessed with what is repeatable. Reality does not surrender itself all at once, it has to be caught in small snatches, over and over again, in a dynamic flickering like the successive frames of a movie film. Such is our attitude.

Albert Camus in one of his early books, *The Myth of Sisyphus,* praised Don Juan as a hero precisely because of his "quantitative" approach to love. He made as many conquests as he possibly could. He practiced the "ethic of quantity."

But Camus was praising Don Juan as a "hero of the absurd" and his ethic of quantity was merely a reflex response to the "essential absurdity" of life. Camus himself later revised his opinion on this matter. The "ethic of quantity" can take effect not only in love but in hate. The Nazi death camps were a perfect example of this ethic of quantity, this "heroism of the absurd." The ethic of quantity leads to Auschwitz and to despair. Camus saw this and there was no further mention of the ethic of quantity in his books after World War II. He moved more and more toward the ethic of love, sacrifice, and compassion.

Anyone who regards love as a deal made on the basis of "needs" is in danger of falling into a purely quantitative ethic. If love is a deal, then who is to say that you should not make as many deals as possible?

From the moment one approaches it in terms of "need" and "fulfillment," love has to be a deal. And what is worse, since we are constantly subjected to the saturation bombing of our senses and imagination with suggestions of impossibly ideal fulfillments, we cannot help revising our estimate of the deal we have made. We cannot help going back on it and making a "better" deal with someone else who is more satisfying.

The situation then is this: we go into love with a sense of immense need, with a naïve demand for perfect fulfillment. After all, this is what we are daily and hourly told to expect. The effect of overstimulation by advertising and other media keeps us at the highest possible pitch of dissatisfaction with the second-rate fulfillment we are actually getting and with the deal we have made. It exacerbates our need. With many people, sexual cravings are kept in a state of high irritation, not by authentic passion, but by the need to prove themselves attractive and successful lovers. They seek security in the repeated assurance that they are still marketable, still a worthwhile product. The long word for all this is narcissism. It has disastrous affects, for it leads people to manipulate each other for selfish ends.

When you habitually function like this, you may seem to be living a very "full" and happy life. You may seem to have everything. You go everywhere, you are in the middle of everything, have lots of friends, "love" and are "loved." You seem in fact to be "perfectly adjusted" sexually and otherwise with your partner(s). Yet underneath there may be a devouring sense that you have nevertheless been cheated, and that the life you are living is not the real thing at all. That is the tragedy of those who are able to measure up to an advertising image which is presented to them on all sides as ideal. Yet they know by experience that there is nothing to it. The whole thing is hollow. They are perhaps in some ways worse off than those who cannot quite make the grade and who therefore always think that perhaps there is a complete fulfillment which they can yet attain. These at least still have hope!

The truth is, however, that this whole concept of life and of love is self-defeating. To consider love merely as a matter of need and fulfillment, as something which works itself out in a cool deal, is to miss the whole point of love, and of life itself.

The basic error is to regard love merely as a need, an appetite, a craving, a hunger which calls for satisfaction. Psychologically, this concept reflects an immature and regressive attitude toward life and toward other people.

To begin with, it is negative. Love is a lack, an emptiness, a nothingness. But it is an emptiness that can be exploited. Others can be drafted into the labor of satisfying this need— provided we cry loud enough and long enough, and in the most effective way. Advertising begins in the cradle! Very often it stays there—and so does love along with it. Psychologists have had some pretty rough things to say about the immaturity and narcissism of love in our marketing society, in which it is reduced to a purely egotistical need that cries out for immediate satisfaction or manipulates others more or less cleverly in order to get what it wants. But the plain truth is this: love is not a matter of getting what you want. Quite the contrary. The insistence on always having what you want, on always being satisfied, on always being fulfilled, makes love impossible. To love you have to climb out of the cradle, where everything is "getting," and grow up to the maturity of giving, without concern for getting anything special in return. Love is not a deal, it is a sacrifice. It is not marketing, it is a form of worship.

In reality, love is a positive force, a transcendent spiritual power. It is, in fact, the deepest creative power in human nature. Rooted in the biological riches of our inheritance, love flowers spiritually as freedom and as a creature response to life in a perfect encounter with another person. It is a living appreciation of life as value and as gift. It responds to the full richness, the variety, the fecundity of living experience itself: it "knows" the inner mystery of life. It enjoys life as an inexhaustible fortune. Love estimates this fortune in a way that knowledge could never do. Love has its own wisdom, its own science, its own way of exploring the inner depths of life in the mystery of the loved person. Love knows, understands, and meets the demands of life insofar as it responds with warmth, abandon, and surrender.

When people are truly in love, they experience far more than just a mutual need for each other's company and consolation. In their relation with each other they become different people: they are more than their everyday selves, more alive, more understanding, more enduring, and seemingly more endowed. They are made over into new beings. They are transformed by the power of their love.

Love is the revelation of our deepest personal meaning, value, and identity. But this revelation remains impossible as long as we are the prisoner of our own egoism. I cannot find myself in myself, but only in another. My true meaning and worth are shown to me not in my estimate of myself, but in the eyes of the one who loves me; and that one must love me as I am, with my faults and limitations, revealing to me the truth that these faults and limitations cannot destroy my worth in *their* eyes; and that I am therefore valuable as a person, in spite of my shortcomings, in spite of the imperfections of my exterior "package." The package is totally unimportant. What matters is this infinitely precious message which I can discover only in my love for another person. And this message, this secret, is not fully revealed to me unless at the same time I am able to see and understand the mysterious and unique worth of the one I love.

This mutual revelation of two persons in their deepest secret is something entirely private. It is their possession, and it cannot be communicated to anyone else until it is embodied in the child who becomes, as it were, a living word, a physical manifestation of their shared secret. Yet in the person of the child the secret remains a mystery known only to the love of the two who participated in the creative surrender which brought the child into being.

Love, then, is a transforming power of almost mystical intensity which endows the lovers with qualities and capacities they never dreamed they could possess. Where do these qualities come from? From the enhancement of life itself, deepened, intensified, elevated, strengthened, and spiritualized by love. Love is not only a special way of being alive, it is the perfection of life. He who loves is more alive and more real than he was when he did not love.

That is perhaps one of the reasons why love seems dangerous: the lover finds in himself too many new powers, too many new insights. Life looks completely different to him, and all his values change. What seemed worthwhile before has become trivial: what seemed impossible has become easy. When a person is undergoing that kind of inner cataclysm, anything might happen. And thank God, it does happen. The world would not be worth much if it didn't!

The power of genuine love is so deep and so strong that it cannot be deflected from its true aim even by the silliest of wrong ideas. When love is alive and mature in a person, it does not matter if he has a false idea of himself and of life: love will guide him according to its own inner truth and will correct his ideas in spite of him. That may be dangerous, but the danger is nothing new and the human race has lived with it for a million-odd years. The trouble is, though, that our wrong ideas may prevent love from growing and maturing in our lives. Once we love, our love can change our thinking. But wrong thinking can inhibit love. Overemphasis on the aspects of need and fulfillment, and obsessions which encourage a self-conscious and narcissistic fixation on one's own pleasure, can easily blight or misdirect the growth of love. That is why the advertising imagery which associates sexual fulfillment with all the most trivial forms of satisfaction—in order to separate the buyer from his dollar—creates a mental and moral climate that is unfavorable to genuine love. Unconsciously the power that should go into creative and positive love for the other person is being short-circuited by images of infantile oral fulfillment and other narcissistic symbols. The lover then becomes the beautiful glowing icon of self-satisfaction, the desirable, slick, and infinitely happy package, rather than the warm presence of one who responds totally to the value and being of the beloved. Even the advertising images of those beatified couples, for whom the years of early middle age are an unending ball, do not convince us of the reality of love: they merely enshrine the cool and consummated deal that our society believes in with superstitious reverence.

What are we going to do about it? Well, for one thing, we can be aware of these immature and inadequate ideas. We do not have to let ourselves be dominated by them. We are free to think in better terms. Of course, we cannot do this all by ourselves. We need the help of articulate voices, themselves taught and inspired by love. This is the mission of the poet, the artist, the prophet. Unfortunately, the confusion of our world has made the message of our poets obscure and our prophets seem to be altogether silent—unless they are devoting their talents to the praise of toothpaste.

Meanwhile, as our media become more sophisticated and more subtle, there is no reason why they should not also create for us a better and saner climate of thought—and present us with a less fallacious fantasy world of symbolic fulfillments.

There is no reason except, of course, that it is easier to make money by exploiting human weakness!

Creative Silence

Imagine a man or a group of people who, alone or together in a quiet place where no radio, no background music can be heard, simply sit for an hour or a half hour in silence. They do not speak. They do not pray aloud. They do not have books or papers in their hands. They are not reading or writing. They are not busy with anything. They simply enter into themselves, not in order to think in an analytical way, not in order to examine, organize, plan, but simply in order to *be*. They want to get themselves together in silence. They want to synthesize, to integrate themselves, to rediscover themselves in a unity of thought, will, understanding, and love that goes beyond words, beyond analysis, even beyond conscious thought. They want to pray not with their lips but with their silent hearts and, beyond that, with the very ground of their being.

What would prompt modern people to do such a thing?

Are they moved by a sense of human need for silence, for reflection, for inner seeking? Do they want to get away from the noise and tension of modern life, at least for a little while, in order to relax their minds and wills and seek a blessed healing sense of inner unity, reconciliation, integration?

These are certainly good enough motives. But for a Christian there are even deeper motives than this. A Christian can realize himself called by God to periods of silence, reflection, meditation, and "listening." We are perhaps too talkative, too activistic, in our conception of the Christian life. Our service of God and of the Church does not consist only in talking and doing. It can also consist in periods of silence, listening, waiting. Perhaps it is very important, in our era of violence and unrest, to rediscover meditation, silent inner unitive prayer, and creative Christian silence.

Silence has many dimensions. It can be a regression and an escape, a loss of self, or it can be presence, awareness, unification, self-discovery. Negative silence blurs and confuses our identity, and we lapse into daydreams or diffuse anxieties. Positive silence pulls us together and makes us realize who we are, who we might be, and the distance between these two. Hence, positive silence implies a disciplined choice, and what Paul Tillich called the "courage to *be*." In the long run, the discipline of creative silence demands a certain kind of faith. For when we come face to face with ourselves in the lonely ground of our own being, we confront many questions about the value of our existence, the reality of our commitments, the authenticity of our everyday lives.

When we are constantly in movement, always busy meeting the demands of our social role, passively carried along on the stream of talk in which people mill around from morning to night, we are perhaps able to escape from our deeper self and from the questions it poses. We can be more or less content with the external identity, the social self, which is produced by our interaction with others in the wheeling and dealing of everyday life. But no matter how honest and open we may be in our relations with others, this social self implies a necessary element of artifice. It is always to some extent a mask. It has to be. Even the American taste for frankness, homely simplicity, affability, plainness, and humor is often a front. Some people are naturally that way. Others educate themselves to play this part in order to be accepted by society. Nor is it entirely pretense: it *appeals* to us. But do we ever give ourselves a chance to realize that this talkative, smiling, perhaps rough-and-ready personage that we seem to be is not necessarily our real self? Do we ever give ourselves a chance to recognize something deeper? Can we face the fact that we are perhaps *not interested* in all this talk and business? When we are quiet, not just for a few minutes, but for an hour or several hours, we may become uneasily aware of the presence within us of a disturbing stranger, the self that is both "I" and someone else. The self that is not entirely welcome in his own house because he is so different from the everyday character that we have constructed out of our dealings with others—and our infidelities in ourselves.

There is a silent self within us whose presence is disturbing precisely because it is so silent: it *can't* be spoken. It has to remain silent. To articulate it, to verbalize it, is to tamper with it, and in some ways to destroy it.

Now let us frankly face the fact that our culture is one which is geared in many ways to help us evade any need to face this inner, silent self. We live in a state of constant semi-attention to the sound of voices, music, traffic, or the generalized noise of what goes on around us all the time. This keeps us immersed in a flood of racket and words, a diffuse medium in which our consciousness is half diluted: we are not quite "thinking," not entirely responding, but we are more or less there. We are not fully *present* and not entirely absent; not fully withdrawn, yet not completely available. It cannot be said that we are really participating in anything and we may, in fact, be half conscious of our alienation and resentment. Yet we derive a certain comfort from the vague sense that we are "part of" something, although we are not quite able to define what that something is—and probably wouldn't want to define it even if we could. We just float along in the general noise. Resigned and indifferent, we share semiconsciously in the mindless mind of Muzak and radio commercials which passes for "reality."

Of course this is not enough to keep us completely forgetful of the other unwelcome self that remains so largely unconscious. The disquieting presence of our deep self keeps forcing its way almost to the surface of awareness. To exorcise this presence we need a more definite stimulation, a distraction, a drink, a drug, a gimmick, a game, a routine of acting out our sense of alienation and trouble. Then it goes away for the time being and we forget who we are.

All of this can be described as "noise," as commotion and jamming which drown out the deep, secret, and insistent demands of the inner self.

With this inner self we have to come to terms *in silence*. That is the reason for choosing silence. In silence we face and admit the gap between the depths of our being, which we consistently ignore, and the surface which is untrue to our own reality. We recognize the need to be at home with ourselves in order that we may go out to meet others, not just with a mask of affability, but with real commitment and authentic love.

If we are afraid of being alone, afraid of silence, it is perhaps because of our secret despair of inner reconciliation. If we have no hope of being at peace with ourselves in our own personal loneliness and silence, we will never be able to face ourselves at all: we will keep running and never stop. And this flight from the self is, as the Swiss philosopher Max Picard pointed out, a "flight from God." After all, it is in the depths of conscience that God speaks, and if we refuse to open up inside and look into those depths, we also refuse to confront the invisible God who is present within us. This refusal is a partial admission that we do not want God to be God any more than we want ourselves to be our true selves.

Just as we have a superficial, external mask which we put together with words and actions that do not fully represent all that is in us, so even believers deal with a God who is made up of words, feelings, reassuring slogans, and this is less the God of faith than the product of religious and social routine. Such a "God" can become a substitute for the truth of the invisible God of faith, and though this comforting image may seem real to us, he is really a kind of idol. His chief function is to protect us against a deep encounter with our true inner self and with the true God.

Silence is therefore important even in the life of faith and in our deepest encounter with God. We cannot always be talking, praying in words, cajoling, reasoning, or keeping up a kind of devout background music. Much of our well-meant interior religious dialogue is, in fact, a smoke screen and an evasion. Much of it is simply self-reassurance and in the end it is little better than a form of self-justification. Instead of really meeting God in the nakedness of faith in which our inmost being is laid bare before him, we act out an inner ritual that has no function but to allay anxiety.

The purest faith has to be tested by silence in which we listen for the unexpected, in which we are open to what we do not yet know, and in which we slowly and gradually prepare for the day when we will reach out to a new level of being with God. True hope is tested by silence in which we have to wait on the Lord in the obedience of unquestioning faith. Isaiah records the word of Yahweh to his rebellious people, who were always abandoning him in order to enter into worthless political and military alliances. "Your safety lies in ceasing to make leagues, your strength is in quiet faith" (Isaiah 20:15), or as another translation has it, "Your salvation lies in conversion and tranquillity, your strength in complete trust." Older texts say "in *silence and hope* shall your strength be." The idea is that faith demands the silencing of questionable deals and strategies. Faith demands the integrity of inner trust which produces wholeness, unity, peace, genuine security. Here we see the creative power and fruitfulness of silence. Not only does silence give us a chance to understand ourselves better, to get a truer and more balanced perspective on our own lives in relation to the lives of others: silence makes us whole if we let it. Silence helps draw together the scattered and dissipated energies of a fragmented existence. It helps us to concentrate on a purpose that really corresponds not only to the deeper needs of our own being but also to God's intentions for us.

This is a really important point. When we live superficially, when we are always outside ourselves, never quite "with" ourselves, always divided and pulled in many directions by conflicting plans and projects, we find ourselves doing many things that we do not really want to do, saying things we do not really mean, needing things we do not really need, exhausting ourselves for what we secretly realize to be worthless and without meaning in our lives: "Why spend your money on what is not food and your earnings on what never satisfies?" (Isaiah 55:2).

The psychologist Erich Fromm has pointed out that this inner contradiction, derived from the alienation and frustration in American life, is one of the roots of violence in our society. We are at odds with ourselves and we seek release by fantasies and dramas of violence. These are simply an amplification of the inner noise and resentment which fill us when we continually ignore the demands of our inmost real self and of God within us.

In many religions the practice of silent meditation has always been given great importance. This is particularly true of Hinduism and Buddhism, where the art of meditation and the cultivation of inner silence are at the heart of everything. But it is also true of Christianity. Catholic monasticism has always stressed the importance of silent meditation on the word of God. The Quakers have always attached great importance to a communal listening to the inner moving of the Spirit. Even Dietrich Bonhoeffer, the apostle of a radical and "secular" Christianity, remarked on the importance of silence. In his prison letters he wrote of his repugnance for the superficial gossip of the prisoners: "Everybody here seems to gossip indiscriminately about his private affairs, no matter whether others show any interest or not, merely for the sake of hearing themselves speak. It is an almost physical urge, but if you manage to suppress it for a few hours, you are afterwards glad you did not let yourself go." And he added that he felt embarrassed by the way men would "demean themselves" just to hear themselves talk. And yet they did not seem preoccupied about the deeper form of expression that would take place if they unburdened themselves to a trusted friend and spoke of what was most intimate in themselves.

What is much more serious is Bonhoeffer's observation that the Church itself engaged in too much empty talk. The Church, in fighting to preserve and assert itself, seemed to him to make self-preservation an end in itself. The Church talked more and more *about* itself and more and more *for* itself, less and less for the Kingdom. He said the Church had "thereby lost its chance to speak a word of reconciliation to mankind and to the world at large." Bonhoeffer foresaw that this would lead the Church—all the churches—into a realm of silence, confusion, and apparent helplessness in which *"traditional language must perforce become powerless and remain silent."* Whether we like it or not, understand it or not, we have now entered into a strange period of desolation and readjustment in which not only the individual Christian but the churches themselves will to a great extent remain silent. There will of course be much resistance to this state of affairs and many will raise their voices louder and louder, not so much to proclaim the Kingdom of God as to make known their own presence and declare that they and their churches are worthy of attention. Bonhoeffer wisely saw that the real purpose of this period of relative silence was a deepening of prayer, a return to the roots of our being, in order that out of silence, prayer, and hope, we might once more receive from God new words and a new way of stating not *our* message but *His*.

"Christianity today will be confined to praying for and doing right by our fellow men. Christian thinking, speaking and organization must be reborn out of this praying and this action." He adds that out of this silent prayer and work will come a whole new language of faith. "We are not yet out of the melting pot and every attempt to hasten matters will only delay the Church's conversion and purgation. It is not for us to prophesy the day, but the day will come when men will be called to utter the word of God with such power as will change and renew the world. It will be a new language which will horrify men and yet overwhelm them by its power . . . a language which proclaims the peace of God with men and the advent of his Kingdom. UNTIL THEN THE CHRISTIAN CAUSE WILL BE A SILENT AND HIDDEN AFFAIR BUT THERE WILL BE THOSE WHO PRAY AND DO RIGHT AND WAIT FOR GOD'S OWN TIME."

The Street Is for Celebration

A city is something you do with space.

A street is a space. A building is an enclosed space. A room is a small enclosed space.

A city is made up of rooms, buildings, streets. It is a crowd of occupied spaces. Occupied or inhabited? Filled or lived in?

The quality of a city depends on whether these spaces are "inhabited" or just "occupied." The character of the city is set by the way the rooms are lived in. The way the buildings are lived in. And what goes on in the streets.

Can a street be an inhabited space?

This may turn out to be a crucial question for a city, for a country, and for the world.

There is a close relation between what goes on in the street and what goes on in the buildings. For instance: Suppose the street is an impersonal no-man's-land: a mere tube through which a huge quantity of traffic is sucked down toward the glass walls where business happens. Suppose the street is a tunnel, a kind of nowhere, something to go through. Something to get out of. Or a nightmare space where you run without getting away.

Then the street cannot be an inhabited space (unless something happens to it). When a street is like a tunnel, a passage, a tube from someplace to someplace else, the people who "live" on it do not really live on it. The street is not where they live but where they have been dumped.

When a street is not inhabited it is a dump.

A street may be a dump for thousands of people who aren't there.

They have been dumped there, but their presence is so provisional they might as well be absent. They occupy space by being displaced in it.

They are out of place in the space allotted to them by society.

They are out of place in small enclosed spaces ("apartments") in which they are constantly reminded that their presence is unimportant and they are unwanted. For instance: waiting for someone to fix the toilet that doesn't work. One week, three weeks, three months. Waiting for the heat. Waiting for the ceiling to fall in. "Oh, yes, I live on X Street." (I am a displaced person who has been dumped in a box on X Street.) (My apartment is uninhabited though there are six of us in it.) (It is not inhabited, just crowded.)

A street where there are thousands of people in this condition is an alienated street. It is a street in a foreign country: yet all the people on it may be natives.

Such a street is always somebody else's street. But whose? The owner is never there. So the building belongs to the landlord? But who is he? Maybe he is a business. So the street belongs to a fiction. (That's why the toilet isn't fixed.) To set the machinery of the big downtown fictions in motion, you have to have that imaginary fluid called money.

Somebody says the street belongs to the city. It is everybody's public street. All right. Is it? You can move around in it under certain conditions. But the conditions are such that you do not feel it is *your* street, because you are not safe, you are not wanted, you are not noticed, you are not liked, and in the end you may just not be allowed.

The street does not even belong to the fuzz. They are no safer on it than anybody else.

Some street!

Can a street be an inhabited space? A space where people enjoy being? A space where people are present to themselves, with full identities, as real people, as happy people?

All right, they sit on the front steps, or sit in the windows, or sit on the fire escapes: but they are sitting there passively watching all the cars go someplace else. Wondering if the people in the cars are the real people. (But those people in the cars: their street is no more inhabited than this street.)

(Do Americans inhabit their vehicles rather than their houses? That is a question. But a car is not a place to live. Or a subway.)

An alienated space, an uninhabited space, is a space where you submit.

You stay where you are put, even though this cannot really be called "living." You stop asking questions about it and you know there is not much point in making any complaint. (Business is not interested in your complaint, only in your rent.) "I live on X Street." Translated: "X Street is the place where I submit, where I give in, where I quit."

(The best thing to do with such a street is pull down the blinds and open a bottle of whiskey.)

Can a street be an inhabited space?

This question begins to take shape. We begin to guess the answer.

To acquire inhabitants, the street will have to be changed. Something must *happen* to the street. Something must be *done to it.* The people who are merely provisionally present, half-absent non-persons must now become really present on the street as *themselves.* They must be recognizable as people. Hence, they must recognize each other as people. (Business is not about to recognize them as people, only as consumers.)

They must be present on the street not simply as candidates for the local shell game, or for manipulation by loan sharks, or for a beating, or for exploitation, or for ridicule, or for total neglect.

Instead of submitting to the street, they must change it.

Instead of being formally and impersonally put in their place by the street, they must transform the street and make it over so that it is livable.

The street can be inhabited if the people on it begin to make their life credible by changing their environment.

Living is more than submission: it is creation.

To live is to create one's own world as a scene of personal happiness.

How do you do that?

Various approaches have been tried.

For instance, you can tear the place apart.

This does, admittedly, have points. It is a way of reminding business, the city, the fuzz, etc., that you are there, that you are tired of being a non-person, that you are not just a passive machine for secreting indefinite amounts of submission. It may get you a TV set or a case of liquor or a new suit. It may even (if the operation is on a larger scale) get you a whole new building. (Though the honeycomb you live in may be replaced by a better one for somebody else.)

But the trouble with this approach is:

—It does not make the street any more habitable.

—It does not make life on this street any more credible.

—It does not make anybody happy.

—It does not change the kind of space the street is.

—It does not not change the city's negative idea of itself and of its streets.

—It accepts the idea that the street is a place going someplace else.

It accepts the street as a tunnel, the city as a rabbit warren. It takes for granted what business and money and the fuzz and everyone else takes for granted: that the street is an impersonal tube for "circulation" of traffic, business, and wealth, so that consequently all the real action is someplace else. That life really happens inside the buildings. But for life to happen inside buildings, it must first find expensive buildings to happen in—downtown or in the suburbs where the money goes along with the traffic.

Violence in the street is all right as an affirmation that one does not submit, but it fails because it accepts the general myth of the street as no-man's-land, as battleground, as no place. Hence, it is another kind of submission. It takes alienation for granted. Merely to fight in the street is to protest, in desperation, that one is unable to change anything. So in the long run it is another way of giving up.

A city is something you do with space.

The first cities of the North American continent were centers for celebration. These were the early Mayan cities of Guatemala and the Zapotecan city of Monte Albán in Mexico.* Very ancient cities of around 500 and 300 B.C., contemporaneous with the city states of Greece. The first Mayan cities and the Zapotecan center of Monte Albán were not the capitals of empires. They did not have armies. They did not

* See *Ishi Means Man: Essays on Native Americans* (Unicorn Press, Greensboro, N.C., 1976), in which Thomas Merton explores this subject more fully. —Ed.

have kings. They did not conquer anyone. Fighting, if any, was on a small scale. The city was not built by war and conquest. Money did not exist. The city was built by the people, not for a king, not for a clique of generals, but for themselves; *it was their place of celebration.*

A lot of work went into those stone pyramids: yet one can say they were built for fun. And for nothing!

When the Mayan pyramids and temples were first built, the people came together in the great open spaces between the buildings. They were dressed in the most beautiful clothes the world has ever seen, made of the bright feathers of paradise birds. They danced, and played a ball game that was also a form of worship, uniting game and ritual. There were as yet no bloody sacrifices (human sacrifice came later with the Toltecs and Aztecs, and military empires).

The first cities of America were spaces marked out for the ample expansion of celebration, joy, worship, play, praise!

In the space of celebration built by the people themselves and for themselves, they came together in joy, in beauty, and each recognized the other as a fellow creator of the common celebration. Their city came alive!

The streets of those cities were not streets in which they watched somebody else going someplace else where all the joy was hidden behind expensive walls. The streets were places where everyone sang together, converging upon the central dance which was the life and identity of the city . . .

Obviously there was something radically different about the way those cities were planned. The streets led to open spaces that were free for everybody, not to closed buildings reserved for the few.

Those early cities knew what to do with space. And what they did with space made human life joyous, real, fully credible. The Bible tells us that in the end it will be like that again, in a city of pure celebration . . .

Meanwhile: what? What about this street?

Can this street become an inhabited space?

Yes, if it can become a place of common celebration.

But we are not pre-classical Mayans and Zapotecans. We did not build our own city. We have been thrown out into this alienated camp of rats, in which we are not wanted, in which we are constantly reminded by everything around us that we are powerless. This city is not built for celebration even though it calls itself "Fun City." Fun is for money. Fun is in buildings where you pay admission.

We can dance in the street, but that will not change the fact that our buildings are lousy, the rent is too high, the garbage is not taken away, and the back yards look like bomb craters.

Never mind. We can begin now to change this street and this city.

We will begin to discover our power to transform our own world.

He who celebrates is not powerless. He becomes a creator because he is a lover.

But celebration is not for the alone.

To pull down the blind and empty the bottle and lie on the floor in a stupor: this may help you to forget the street for a while, but it is a surrender. It is the crowning submission, the acceptance of powerlessness, willingness to admit you are a nothing. The alienated city isolates men from one another in despair, lovelessness, defeat. It is crowded with people who are not present to each other: it is like a desert, although it is full of people.

Celebration is not noise. It is not a spinning head. It is not just individual kicks.

It is the creation of a common identity, a common consciousness.

Celebration is everybody making joy.

Not as a duty (you can't manufacture joy out of the duty to have fun).

Celebration is when we let joy make itself out of our love.

We like to be together. We like to dance together. We like to make pretty and amusing things. We like to laugh at what we have made. We like to put bright colors on the walls—more bright colors on ourselves. We like our pictures, they are crazy. Celebration is crazy: the craziness of not submitting even though "they," "the others," the ones who make life impossible, seem to have all the power. Celebration is the beginning of confidence, therefore of power.

When we laugh at them, when we celebrate, when we make our lives beautiful, when we give one another joy by loving, by sharing, then we manifest a power they cannot touch. We can be the artisans of a joy they never imagined.

We can build a fire of happiness in this city that will put them to shame.

They with their gold have turned our lives into rubble. But we with love will set our lives on fire and turn the rubble back into gold. This time the gold will have real worth. It will not be just crap that came out of the earth. It will be the infinite value of human identity flaming up in a heart that is confident in loving. That is the beginning of power. That is the beginning of the transformation. One day, you'll see!

Meanwhile, we have an answer to the question:

Can the street become an inhabited space?
Yes, when it becomes a space for celebration.

Symbolism: Communication
or Communion?

The topic announced in this title could easily lend itself to a detailed, long-winded academic treatment. In order to avoid the disadvantages of such an approach, the author will permit himself to set down, in a more spontaneous and less organized form, a few bare intuitions. These may suggest further lines of thought in the mind of the reader.

In dealing with symbolism one enters an area where reflection, synthesis, and contemplation are more important than investigation, analysis, and science. One cannot apprehend a symbol unless one is able to awaken, in one's own being, the spiritual resonances which respond to the symbol not only as *sign* but as "sacrament" and "presence." Needless to say, when we speak of symbol here we are interested only in the full and true sense of the word. Mere conventional symbols, more or less arbitrarily taken to represent something else, concrete images which stand for abstract qualities, are not symbols in the highest sense. The true symbol does not merely point to some hidden object. It contains in itself a structure which in some way makes us aware of the inner meaning of life and of reality itself. A true symbol takes us to the center of the circle, not to another point on the circumference. A true symbol points to the very heart of all being, not to an incident in the flow of becoming.

One might begin by asking whether one can even attempt such reflections, in the Western world of the twentieth century, without a certain note of urgency, accompanied by a sense of conflict and confusion. In other words, the reader must be prepared to find these remarks somewhat lacking in serenity. The tension in the West, especially in America, between a naïve surface optimism (belief in scientific progress as an end in itself) and the deep, savage destructive tendencies of a technology and an economy in which man becomes the instrument of blind inhuman forces makes us realize that the *degradation of the sense of symbolism* in the modern world is one of its many alarming symptoms of spiritual decay.

The most unique and disturbing feature of this spiritual degeneration is that it finds itself armed with a colossal will-to-power and with almost unlimited facilities for implementing its brutal aspirations. Thus twentieth-century man who mistakenly imagines himself to be standing on a peak of civilized development (since he confuses technology with civilization) does not realize that he has in reality reached a critical point of moral and spiritual disorganization. He is a savage armed not with a club or a spear but with the most sophisticated arsenal of diabolical engines, to which new inventions are added every week.

Nietzsche's declaration that "God is dead" is one that is now taken up, not without seriousness, by the prophets of the most "progressive" tendencies in Western religion, which now seems, in some quarters, eager to prove its sincerity, in the eyes of a godless society, by an act of spiritual self-destruction.

Meanwhile, artists, poets, and others who might be expected to have some concern with the inner life of man are declaring that the reason why God has ceased to be present to man (therefore "dead") is that man has ceased to be present to himself, and that consequently the true significance of the statement "God is dead" is really that "MAN is dead." The obvious fact of man's material agitation and external frenzy serves only to emphasize his lack of spiritual life.

Since it is by symbolism that man is spiritually and consciously in contact with his own deepest self, with other men, and with God, then both the "death of God" and the "death of man" are to be accounted for by the fact that symbolism is dead. The death of symbolism is itself the most eloquent and significant symbol in our modern cultural life. Since man cannot live without signs of the invisible, and since his capacity to apprehend the visible and the invisible as a meaningful unity depends on the creative vitality of his symbols, then, even though he may claim to have no further interest in this "bringing together" (which is the etymological sense of "symbol"), man will nevertheless persist in spite of himself in making symbols. If they are not living signs of creative integration and inner life, then they will become morbid, decaying, and pathogenic signs of his own inner disruption. The solemn vulgarity, indeed the spiritually hideous and sometimes unconsciously obscene nature of some of the "symbols" that are still held worthy of respect by the establishment and by the masses (whether in the capitalist West or in socialist countries), has naturally aroused the total protest of the modern artist who now creates only anti-art and non-symbol, or else contemplates without tremor and without comment the ultimate spiritual affront of those forms and presences which marketing and affluence have made "normal" and "ordinary" everywhere.

The loss of the sense of symbol in scientific and technological society is due in part to an incapacity to distinguish between the *symbol* and the *indicative sign*. The function of the sign is communication, and first of all, the communication of factual or practical knowledge. The function of the symbol is not the statement of facts or the conveyance of information, even of spiritual information about absolute or religiously revealed truths. A symbol does not merely teach and inform. Nor does it *explain*.

It is quite true that the content of a religious symbol is usually rich with spiritual or revealed truth. Nevertheless, revelation and spiritual vision are contained in symbols not in order that one may extract them from the symbol and study them or appropriate them intellectually apart from the symbol itself. Revealed truth is made present concretely and existentially in symbols, and is grasped in and with the symbol by a living response of the subject. This response defies exact analysis and cannot be accurately described to one who does not experience it authentically in himself. The capacity for such experience is developed by living spiritual traditions and by contact with a spiritual master (*guru*), or at least with a vital and creative liturgy and a traditional doctrine. So, to demand that a symbol should fulfill the function of informing and explaining, or clarifying and scientifically verifying all the most intimate facts of the cosmos, of man, of man's place in the cosmos, of man's relation to God, of man's relation to himself, and so on, is to demand that the symbol should do what indicative or quantitative signs do. As soon as one makes such a demand, he immediately becomes convinced that the symbol is of far less practical value than the sign. In a world where practical use and quantitative scientific information are highly prized, the symbol quickly becomes meaningless.

When the symbol is called upon to *communicate,* it necessarily restricts itself to conveying the most trivial kind of idea or information. The symbol is then reduced to the *trademark* or the *political badge,* a mere sign of identification. Identification is not identity. "Rubber stamp" identification is actually a diminution or loss of identity, a submersion of identity in the generalized class. The pseudosymbols of the mass movement become signs of the pseudomystique in which the mass man loses his individual self in the false, indeed the demonic void, the general pseudoself of the Mass Society. The symbols of the Mass Society are crude and barbaric rallying points for emotion, fanaticism, and exalted forms of hatred masking as moral indignation. The symbols of Mass Society are ciphers on the face of a moral and spiritual void.

Werner Heisenberg, the physicist, has discussed the revolutionary change in man's attitude toward nature in an age of science and technology.* In the pre-scientific era man sought even in his "scientific" investigations to arrive at the most living and most qualitatively significant apprehension of nature as a whole. Such an apprehension, even when it contained elements of experiment and objective observation, remained essentially poetic, philosophical, and even religious.

Modern science does not seek to create a "living representation" but to acquire and coordinate quantitative data

* All quotations from Werner Heisenberg in this section are from his essay "The Representation of Nature in Contemporary Physics" (1954).

from which to construct explanations or simply working hypotheses with a practical orientation. Where religion, philosophy, and poetry use the power of the creative symbol to attain a synthetic apprehension of life in its ultimate metaphysical roots, science uses technical instruments to gather quantitative data about the physical universe, and those data are reduced to mathematical formulas, which can then serve the practical needs of technology.

What is not generally realized yet is that modern science itself has undermined the world view of naïve materialism which believed that "ultimate reality" could be found in the elementary particles of matter. Science has above all destroyed the materialistic idea of a purely objective knowledge in which we can, with absolute certitude, make statements about "reality" based on our observations of matter, as if we ourselves were observing everything from a platform of "science" in a pure realm of truth. Actually, as Heisenberg says, we cannot observe the particles of matter as pure objects, since the fact of our observation itself enters into the interaction and behavior of the entities we observe. Hence it is that the formulas of the atomic physicist represent *"no longer the behavior of the elementary particles but rather our knowledge of this behavior."* At the same time, technology as it develops and apparently "penetrates" the "mysteries of nature," in so doing *"transforms our environment and impresses our image upon it."* This use of technology and science to transform nature and bring it under man's power appears to Heisenberg an extension of biological processes, so that man's technology becomes part of him as the spider's web is inseparable from the biology of the spider. The result of this is that man no longer stands in opposition to nature; he confronts no adversary in the world in which he is alone with himself and which he will soon completely transform in his own image.

But the problem arises: there does remain one adversary, *man himself,* and as Heisenberg says, in this situation man's technology, instead of broadening and expanding man's capacities for life, suddenly threatens to contract them and even destroy them altogether. "In such a confrontation, the extension of technology need no longer be an indication of progress."

Now symbolism exercises its vital and creative function in a cosmos where man had to come to terms with a nature in which he was struggling to maintain a place of his own—albeit a place of spiritual preeminence. Symbolism strives to "bring together" man, nature, and God in a living and sacred synthesis. But technological man finds himself in another artificial synthesis in which he has no longer any knowledge of anything except himself, his machines, and his knowledge that he knows what he knows. This knowledge is not a knowledge of reality but a knowledge of knowledge. That is to say—man no longer is "in contact with nature" but is only well situated in the context of his own experiments. He can say with certainty how an experiment will turn out, but he cannot find any ultimate meaning for this. Man is, therefore, cut off from any reality except that of his own processes—that is to say, in fact, of his own inner chaos—and that of the extraordinary new world of his machines. As the knowledge of his own disruption is unpalatable, he turns more and more to his machines. But through the power of his machines he acts out the uncomprehended tragedy of his inner disruption. As Heisenberg says, in the arresting comparison, "man finds himself in the position of a captain whose ship has been so securely built of iron and steel that his compass no longer points to the north but only towards the ship's mass of iron."

Heisenberg quotes the Chinese sage, Chuang Tzu, who, twenty-five hundred years ago, discovered that dependence even on a simple kind of machine caused man to become "uncertain in his inner impulses." Naturally, the advance of science and technology is irreversible and man now has to come to terms with himself in his new situation. He cannot do so if he builds an irrational and unscientific faith on the absolute and final objectivity of scientific knowledge of nature. The limits of science must be recognized and blind faith in an uncontrolled proliferation in technology must be abjured.

To return to the ship's captain, Heisenberg says that his danger will be less if he recognizes what has gone wrong and tries to navigate by some other means—for instance, by the stars. To "navigate by the stars" he needs to go beyond the limitation of a scientific world view and recover his sense of the symbol.

Alfred North Whitehead, who, as a scientist, took a cool and detached view of symbolism, declared that society needed to defend itself against the proliferation of symbols which "have a tendency to run wild like the vegetation of a tropical forest." It is certainly true that a mass of obscure symbols that have ceased to illuminate and invigorate may end by stifling social and personal life. Therefore, "an occasional revolution in symbolism is required," says Whitehead, in a rather offhand way, as if symbols could be created anew by act of Parliament. Nevertheless, Whitehead is quite definite in saying, "Symbolism is no mere idle fancy or corrupt degeneration: it is inherent in the very texture of human life." He sees clearly that symbolism does not seek merely to convey information but to enhance the importance and value of what it symbolizes (see his *Symbolism, Its Meaning and Efficacy*). He points out how in social life symbolism replaces "the force of instinct which suppresses individuality" and creates instead a dynamism of thought and action in which the individual person can integrate his own free activity into the work of the common-weal, without simply submitting, in passive and automatic fashion, to external directives of authority.

By means of the social symbol, the person can make the common good really his own. By means of the religious symbol, the person can enter into communion, not only with his fellow man and with all creation, but with God. Symbolism is powerful, says Whitehead, because of its "enveloping suggestiveness and emotional efficacy." However, the symbol is not merely emotional, and "it affords a foothold for reason by its delineation of the particular instinct which it expresses."

Whitehead, however, thinking in terms of the mass movement and of blind political prejudice, points to the danger of those (political) symbols which evoke a *direct (reflex) response* without reference to any meaning whatever. The effect of such symbols becomes hypnotic—certain responses, usually violent, are elicited without thought and without moral judgment.

Thus, in certain unhealthy situations, the political or military symbol can produce the automatic obedience of storm troopers and political policemen who are ready for any savagery and any abomination. The symbol, in this case, has the effect of suppressing conscience and reasoned judgment and bringing about a demonic communion in evil.

But is this the fault of symbolism as such? Certainly not. It is due to the degradation of symbols. A man who is trained to respond to higher, more creative, and more spiritual symbols will *instantly react in revulsion* against the crude barbarity of the totalist symbol. His reaction, too, is instinctive and, as it were, automatic. What matters, then, is not that the symbol tends to concentrate around itself man's instinctive forces for action and self-dedication, but that living and creative symbols elevate and direct that action in a good sense, while pathogenic and depraved symbols divert man's energies to evil and destruction.

The point is to educate men so that they can discern one from the other.

But if in our education we assume that all symbolism is mere fantasy and illusion, we no longer teach people to make this distinction. Hence, while imagining they have risen above the "childishness" of symbolism, they will easily and uncritically submit, in fact, to the fascination of the perverse and destructive symbols which are actually obsessing the whole society in which they live.

In our modern world the fascination of violence has become, through TV, magazines, movies, radio, etc., almost irresistible. There is now so much free-floating terror and hatred in the moral climate of the world that the slightest and most ridiculous of actions can be interpreted symbolically and instantly unleash mass hysteria on a global scale. The only remedy for this is in a return to the level of spiritual wisdom on which the higher symbols operate. This is easy enough to say: but is it actually possible today? Have we, in fact, simply fallen away from our capacity for "symbolically conditioned action" in the higher sense (guidance by the *meaning* and *wisdom* of the higher symbol) and relapsed into purely reflex and instinctive action without reference to meaning, and above all *without any rational sense of causality and responsibility?*

At the end of his suggestive essay, without perhaps fully intending to do so, Whitehead speaks of the community life of ants governed (probably) by pure instinct rather than by meaningful symbol.

It is no new idea to say that if man does survive in his cybernetic society without blowing himself up, it may well be that, renouncing the creative symbol and living mechanically, he learns to make his world into a vast anthill. If mere survival is all we desire, this may seem a satisfactory prospect. But if our vocation is to share creatively in the spiritualization of our existence, then the anthill concept is somewhat less than desirable.

Obviously the direction that symbolism must take is that of expressing union, understanding, and love among men— what Paul Tillich has called a "communal eros." But the crude symbolism of violence has gained its power precisely from the fact that the symbolism of love has been so terribly debased, cheapened, and dehumanized. There is something very frightening about the awful caricature of love and beauty which has manifested itself for several centuries, growing progressively worse, in Western literature and art, including religious literature and art, until today the sensitive mind recoils entirely from the attempt to see and portray "the beautiful" and concentrates on the hideous, the meaningless, the formless, in a sincere attempt to clear the desecrated sanctuary of the rubbish which fills it.

In technological society, in which the means of communication and signification have become fabulously versatile, and are at the point of an even more prolific development, thanks to the computer with its inexhaustible memory and its capacity for immediate absorption and organization of facts, the very nature and use of communication itself becomes unconsciously symbolic. Though he now has the capacity to communicate anything, anywhere, instantly, man finds himself with *nothing to say*. Not that there are not many things he could communicate, or should attempt to communicate. He should, for instance, be able to meet with his fellow man and discuss ways of building a peaceful world. He is incapable of this kind of confrontation. Instead of this, he has intercontinental ballistic missiles which can deliver nuclear death to tens of millions of people in a few moments. This is the most sophisticated message modern man has, apparently, to convey to his fellow man. It is, of course, a message about himself, his alienation from himself, and his inability to come to terms with life.

The vital role of the symbol is precisely this: to express and to encourage man's acceptance of his own center, his own ontological roots in a mystery of being that transcends his individual ego. But when man is reduced to his empirical self and confined within its limits, he is, so to speak, excluded from himself, cut off from his own roots, condemned to spiritual death by thirst and starvation in a wilderness of externals. In this wilderness there can be no living symbols, only the dead symbols of dryness and destruction which bear witness to man's own inner ruin. But he cannot "see" these symbols, since he is incapable of interior response.

In a recent essay, of a rather esoteric yet popular nature, an American theoretician of nuclear war devised an elaborate "ladder of escalation" in which his avowed purpose was to construct a *rudimentary language*. It is a language of destruction, in which each rung on the "ladder" (including massive exchanges of nuclear weapons, destruction of cities, missile sites, etc.) was a way of "saying something" and of "conveying information" to the enemy. One feels that millennia ago, in the early Stone Age, communication among men must have been more basic, more articulate, and more humane. The "ladder" (itself an ancient symbol, as in Genesis 28:12, as in Babylonian religion, as in the cosmic tree, the *axis mundi* of Asian myths, etc.) has now become a symbol of the total and negative futility of a huge technological machine organized primarily for destruction. At the top of the ladder is not God but "Spasm." But "spasm" is on every rung. All rungs of escalation are "insensate war."

Of course, the more constant and more public claim made by the salesmen of communication is that our modern media are still interested, first of all, in rapidly conveying messages of love. This, of course, is another way of affirming what is, in fact, so universally doubted: that men still have messages of genuine love to convey. Let us, for a moment, not dispute this. Here is one instance of such "communication."

A busy physician in an American city has a telephone in his car, so that even when he is not in his office, at the hospital, or at home, he can receive urgent calls. While he is driving through the city, his phone rings and he picks it up. It is a call from Africa, via shortwave radio. He listens. It is a friend who has recently gone to Africa. What does he have to say? Nothing. "I had a chance to make this call for nothing so I thought I would say 'Hello.' " They exchange greetings, they assure each other that they are well, their families are well, and so on. They indulge in the same completely inconsequential kind of talk as in any other casual phone call. One can reflect on this and recognize that even some of the seemingly "important" matters that occupy the communications media are perhaps almost as trivial as this.

Someone will argue: what does it matter if they had no really serious information to communicate? This was something more than communication. It was an expression of friendship, therefore of love. Is not love more important than factual information? Were these friends not seeking *communion* even more than communication?

To this one can only answer that love and communion are

indeed most important and far outweigh mere "communication." But the fact remains that where communion is no longer understood, and where, in fact, communication is regarded as primary, because "practical," then people are reduced to making a *symbolically useless* use of expensive means of communication, in an effort to achieve communion. But the symbolic uselessness remains self-frustrating, since, in the code of a technological culture, to carry out such useless acts is to become guilty of a sin against the basic virtue: practicality.

Yet even here there are most curious ambiguities, for while the extraordinary efficacy of technological instruments increases every day, one is obliged to admit that the uses to which they are put are increasingly useless and even destructive. What is the uselessness of a friendly phone call from Africa to America compared to the titanic uselessness of space travel and moon flights? One suddenly realizes that, in point of fact, technology at present is built entirely on uselessness rather than on use, and this uselessness is in fact symbolic. (It is a symptom. And in a sickness, a symptom is a symbol. Right understanding of the symptom can lead to restoration of health. Wrong response aggravates the illness.) The one great usefulness technology might have for us is precisely what no one sees: its symbolic uselessness, which no amount of sermons on progress can manage to justify.

Traditionally, the value of the symbol is precisely in its apparent uselessness as a means of simple communication. *Because it is not an efficient mode of communicating information, the symbol can achieve a higher purpose, the purpose of going beyond practicality and purpose, beyond cause and effect.* Instead of establishing a new contact by a meeting of minds in the sharing of news, the symbol tells nothing new:

it revives our awareness of what we already know, but deepens that awareness. What is "new" in the symbol is the ever new discovery of a new depth and a new actuality in what IS and always has been. The function of the symbol is not merely to *bring about* a union of minds and wills, as a cause produces an effect; the function of the symbol is to manifest a union that *already exists but is not fully realized*. The symbol awakens awareness, or restores it. Therefore, it aims not at communication but at communion. Communion is the awareness of participation in an ontological or religious reality: in the mystery of being, of human love, of redemptive mystery, of contemplative truth.

The purpose of the symbol, if it can be said to have a "purpose," is not to increase the quantity of our knowledge and information but to deepen and enrich the *quality* of life itself by bringing man into communion with the mysterious sources of vitality and meaning, of creativity, love, and truth, to which he cannot have direct access by means of science and technique. The realm of symbol is the realm of wisdom in which man finds truth not only in and through objects but in himself and in his life, lived in accordance with the deepest principles of divine wisdom. Naturally, such wisdom does not exclude knowledge of objects. It gives a new dimension to science. What would our world of science be, if only we had wisdom?

Appreciation of the symbol necessarily implies a certain view of reality itself, a certain cosmology and a religious metaphysic of being, above all a spiritual view of man. Symbols begin to have a living and creative significance only when man is understood to be a sacred being. The "desecration" of man begins when symbols are emptied of meaning and are allowed to survive precisely insofar as they are patronizingly admitted to be misleading but still "necessary for the ignorant."

The symbol is then regarded only as a politically or religiously "useful lie," insofar as it seems to communicate information on a childish level, information which is inadequate but acceptable to those to whom "objective truth" is not yet clear. The "sacredness" of man consists, however, precisely in the fact that the truth for which and by which he lives is primarily within himself, and therefore prime importance belongs to the symbol which directs him to this truth, not as an external object, but as a spiritual and personal fulfillment. Without this interior fulfillment, the mind of man is not equipped to cope with objective truth, and the spirit that has no interior roots will find that its "scientific" knowledge of objects turns out to be "a lie" even when it is materially correct. It completely misleads him as to the meaning of his own existence.

Thus, in order that man be profoundly secularized and "desecrated," symbols themselves must be discredited and excluded from art, culture, and religion. For Marx, the symbol (above all, the religious symbol) is nothing but an instrument of alienation. Yet how many pseudoreligious symbols have sprung up in Marxist society, equaling in vulgarity and in triviality those of the capitalist and fascist societies? The emptiness of these symbols bears witness to the alienation of man in these societies.

The desecration of symbols has been systematically proceeding for two centuries and more, especially in semiscientific theories of anthropology, archaeology, comparative religion, and so on. For example, consider the totally unrealistic theory that the art of primitive man had its origin in a utilitarian concept, the supposed magic efficacy of an artistic image. To paint a picture of a bison on the wall of a cave was supposedly primitive man's way of saying that he was desperately hungry and had not tasted bison meat for a long time. He painted a bison on the theory that the image gave him power over a real bison. The painting constituted a "virtual capture" of the desired prey. Once again, the symbol is seen only as an efficacious sign, an attempt to exercise causality, to produce a practical and useful effect in the world of objects. This means that primitive art is understood only in modern commercial and technological terms.

A symbol is thought, like other signs, to have only a practical reference. It is supposed to claim a certain kind of efficacy, to pretend to a definite causal influence: it provides a mode of control over objects. It is part of a technique. It is to be seen in a context of magic and archaic pre-technology which is now discarded as totally inefficacious. Art is, then, seen only as an imitation of objects, as a substitute for the possession of a desired object. What is important is not the art but the object to which it points. This is the basic axiom of advertising, which *suggests* a need, awakens a need, and keeps it awake, in the prospective consumer, by means of "art." This is also the principle governing political propaganda art.

This crude theory of the origin of primitive art lacks, first of all, any appreciation for the *extraordinary creative power* of these amazing symbols made by prehistoric man. The most elementary familiarity with modern psychology ought to be enough to show that such creative power could not normally proceed from a naked physical desire. It could only come from a sublimated transformation of desire.

Acquaintance with primitive religion shows us that primitive man had a deep sense of kinship with the animals among which he lived, including those on which he depended for his existence. His "love" for the bison or the reindeer was some-

thing far deeper and more complex than a modern city dwell-
er's craving for this or that kind of meat, derived from an
animal never seen in its natural state. This primitive "love"
of the animals was embodied in a very complex religious
relationship, hedged in with severe ritual limitations which
prohibited useless and irresponsible killing and all kinds of
misuse. Primitive art was far from being merely a weak, inefficacious, half-despairing attempt of an inept hunter to bring
down good luck on his spear. It was also an acknowledgment
of a deep communion with all living beings, with the animals
among which man lived on terms of familiarity that are no
longer imaginable to us.

Hence, the symbols of primitive art are vitally significant
on more than one level. There is, of course, the representation
of the everyday level, the hunt for food. But there is also
another level, that of kinship, of religious fellowship with the
animal regarded from one point of view as superior to man,
as "divine."

The Biblical polemic against the deification of natural beings and forces comes relatively late in man's cultural development, and doubtless by that time primitive religion had, in
fact, become deeply degenerate. But a study of the philosophical ideas of the Bantu in Africa still shows that primitive
man's reverence for life and for the sacred, creative dynamism
of life, expressed in his art and in his symbolism, could be
extremely deep and pure. Modern man's misinterpretation
of his primitive ancestors' thought and culture reflects discredit on our own blind complacency and sense of superiority.

Primitive art undoubtedly draws a great deal of its power
from the *ambivalence of love and guilt,* due to the fact that
man had to slay a loved, admired, and mysterious object in
order to keep alive himself. This became so strong that, eventually, in certain highly developed religious cultures, such as
those of India, the killing of animals and the eating of meat

were eventually prohibited. Here one encounters an even deeper level of communion: the level of *being itself*. Man and the animal are finally seen as sharing in the ontological mystery of being; they are somehow one "in God the Creator." Or as Hinduism would say, the Atman is one in them both.

Primitive art cannot be comprehended unless the implications of these different levels of symbolic meaning are somehow apprehended. Merely to declare that primitive art had a magic or utilitarian purpose, aimed at a limited, practical result, is to ignore this symbolic quality and attach oneself exclusively to a supposed causal signification which is then shown to be so naïve and preposterous that it cannot be taken seriously. Thus, substituting the practical sign for the religious symbol, the theorist manages to call into question all forms of culture—religious, philosophical, artistic, mystical—which make use of the symbol. All instantly become incomprehensible.

Paul Tillich, the American Protestant theologian I have already mentioned, has rightly seen that "a real symbol points to an object that can never become an object." This is a profound and intriguing declaration. The symbol cannot possibly convey *information about an object* if it is true to its nature as symbol. Only when it is debased does a symbol point exclusively to an object other than itself. *The symbol is an object pointing to the subject.* The symbol is not an object for its own sake: it is a reminder that we are summoned to a deeper spiritual awareness, far beyond the level of subject and object.

It would, however, be a great mistake to think that the symbol merely reminds the subject to become aware of himself as object, after the Western manner of introspection and self-examination. We must repeat, the symbol is an object which leads beyond the realm of division where subject and object stand over against one another. That is why the symbol goes beyond communication to communion. Communication takes place between subject and object, but communion is beyond the division: it is a sharing in basic unity. This does not necessarily imply a "pantheist metaphysic." Whether or not they may be strictly monistic, the higher religions all point to this deeper unity, because they all strive after the experience of this unity. They differ, sometimes widely, in ways of explaining what this unity is and how one may attain to it.

Christianity sees this unity as a special gift of God, a work of grace, which brings us to unity with God and one another in the Holy Spirit. The religions of Asia tend to see this unity in an ontological and natural principle in which all beings are metaphysically one. The experience of unity for the Christian is unity "in the Holy Spirit." For Asian religions it is unity in Absolute Being (Atman) or in the Void (Sunyata). The difference between the two approaches is the difference between an ontologist mysticism and a theological revelation: between a return to an Absolute Nature and surrender to a Divine Person.

The symbols of the higher religions may at first sight seem to have little in common. But when one comes to a better understanding of those religions, and when one sees that the experiences which are the fulfillment of religious belief and practice are most clearly expressed in symbols, one may come to recognize that often the symbols of different religions may have more in common than the abstractly formulated official doctrines.

The Chinese ideogram *Chung* (中) bears more than a superficial resemblance to the Cross. It is also a picture of the five cosmic points, the four cardinal points centered on the "pivot" of Tao. This is analogous to the traditional Christian cosmic interpretation of the Cross symbol, the "picture" of the new creation and of the recapitulation of all in Christ (Ephesians 1:12). One might pursue these analogies in studying the traditional Buddhist stupas, and so on. It is sufficient to suggest those lines of thought which the reader can investigate for himself.

A symbol is, then, not simply an indicative sign conveying information about a religious object, a revelation, a theological truth, a mystery of faith. It is an *embodiment* of that truth, a "sacrament," by which one participates in the religious presence of the saving and illuminating One. It does not merely point the way to the One as object. As long as the One is regarded as object, it is not the One, it is dual or multiple, since there is a division between It and the one (or ones) seeking to attain it. Hence, the question of a Zen master: "If all things return to the one, where does the one return to?" To such a question there can be no answer, since the question itself is contradictory. Reason might seek a way to get around the contradiction and resolve it. Symbol tends rather to accept the contradiction in order to point beyond it. It seems to take the One as if it were an object, but, in fact, it reveals the One as present within our own subjective and interior entity. It reveals that the subjectivity of the subject is, in fact, now, deeply rooted in the infinite God, the Father, the Word, the Spirit, or in Hindu terms Atman, *sat-cit-ananda*. The symbol does not merely bridge the distance and cause the believer to become united with God. It proclaims that, in one way or another, according to the diversity of religions, the believer can and does even now return to Him

from Whom he first came. It does not simply promise a new
and effective communication by which the believer can make
himself heard by the Deity and can even exercise a certain
persuasive force upon Him. It does much more: it opens the
believer's inner eye, the eye of the heart, to the realization
that he must come to be centered in God because that, in fact,
is where his center is. He must become what he is, a "son of
God," "seeking only his Father's will," abandoned to the
invisible Presence and Nearness of Him Who Is, for there is
no reality anywhere else but in Him.

But the symbol also speaks to many believers in one: it
awakens them to their communion with one another in God.
It does not merely bring their minds into communication with
one another, in a common worship, for instance. Worship
itself is symbolic, and as such it is communion rather than
communication. (Hence the great pity of a certain type of
Christianity, which has become in great measure mere communication of information, a meeting where the audience is
entertained by an inspiring lecture.) Worship is symbolic
communion in mystery, the mystery of the actual presence
of Him Who is Being, Light, and Blessedness of Love. It is
recognition of the fact that, in reality, we cannot be without
Him, that we are centered in Him, that He dwells in us, and
that because He is in us and we in Him, we are one with one
another in Him.

. . . that all may be one, even as thou, Father, in me and I in
thee; that they also may be one in us, that the world may believe
that thou hast sent me. And the glory that thou hast given me, I
have given to them, that they may be one, even as we are one: I
in them and thou in me; that they may be perfected in unity, and
that the world may know that thou hast sent me, and that thou
hast loved them even as thou hast loved me.

Father, I will that where I am, they also whom thou has given me may be with me; in order that they may behold my glory, which thou hast given me, because thou hast loved me before the creation of the world.

JOHN 17:21–24.

The desecration of symbols cannot be blamed exclusively on the forces of secularism and atheism. On the contrary, it unfortunately began in religious circles themselves. When a tradition loses its contemplative vitality and wisdom, its symbolism gradually loses its meaning and ceases to be a point of contact with "the center." Symbolism degenerates into allegorism. The symbol has no life of its own, it merely designates an abstraction. In the system of allegories, everything points to everything else and nothing conclusively ends in real meaning. There is nothing but a circle of references without end. "A" points to "B," which points to "C," which points to "A." The center is forgotten.

All that matters is to have a key to the hidden meanings and to know that "A" really stands for "B," so that when you say "A" you really mean "B." But then a scientific critic comes along and says that "A" does not mean "B"; that there is no way of knowing that "A" means anything at all; and all we can say is, that in 500 B.C. "A" was thought to mean "B," while today science shows this interpretation to be impossible.

When the symbol degenerates into a mere means of communication and ceases to be a sign of communion, it becomes an idol, insofar as it seems to point to an object with which it brings the subject into effective, quasi-magical, psychological, or parapsychological communication. It would be pointless here to go into the ancient Biblical polemic against "idols of wood and stone." There are much more dangerous and much more potent idols in the world today: signs of cosmic and technological power, political and scientific idols, idols of the

nation, the party, the race. These are evident enough, but the
fact that they are evident in themselves does not mean that
people do not submit more and more blindly, more and more
despairingly to their complete power. The idol of national
military strength was never more powerful than today, even
though men claim to desire peace. In fact, though they pay
lip service to the love of life and of humanity, they obscurely
recognize that in submitting to the demon of total war they
are, in fact, releasing themselves from the anxieties and per-
plexities of a "peace" that is fraught with too many ambiguities for comfort. Can man resist the temptation to sacrifice
himself utterly and irrevocably to this idol?

Another idol that is not so obvious is that of supposed "spiritual experience" sought as an object and as an end in itself.
Here, too, the temptation that offers itself is one of escape
from anxiety and limitation, and an *affirmation of the individual self as object,* but as a special kind of object, *to be
experienced as free from all limitations.*

The temptation of modern pseudomysticism is perhaps one
of the gravest and most subtle, precisely because of the confusion it causes in the minds and hearts of those who might
conceivably be drawn to authentic communion with God and
with their fellow men by the austere traditional ways of obedience, humility, sacrifice, love, knowledge, worship, meditation, and contemplation. All these ancient ways demand the
control and the surrender, the ultimate "loss" of the empirical
self in order that we may be "found" again in God. But
pseudomysticism centers upon the individualistic enjoyment
of experience, that is, upon *the individual self experienced as
without limitation.* This is a sublime subtlety by which one
can eat one's cake and have it. It is the discovery of a spiritual
trick (which is sought as a supremely valuable "object") in

which, while seeming to renounce and deny oneself, one, in fact, definitively affirms the ego as a center of indefinite and angelic enjoyments. One rests in the joy of the spiritualized self, very much aware of one's individual identity and of one's clever achievement in breaking through to a paradise of delights without having had to present one's ticket at the entrance. The ticket that must be surrendered is one's individual, empirical ego. Pseudomysticism, on the contrary, seeks the permanent delight of the ego in its own spirituality, its own purity, as if it were itself absolute and infinite.

And this explains the success and the danger of the current Western fad for producing "spiritual experience" by means of drugs.

Shall we conclude on a note of pessimism? Not necessarily. The present crisis of man is something for which we have no adequate historical standard of comparison. Our risks are extreme. The hopes which we have based on our technological skill are very probably illusory. But there remain other dimensions. The fact that we are not able to grasp these dimensions is not necessarily cause for despair. If our destiny is not entirely in our own hands, we can still believe, as did our fathers, that our lives are mysteriously guided by a wisdom and a love which can draw the greatest good out of the greatest evil. The fact remains that man needs to recognize something of this mysterious guidance and enter into active cooperation with it. But such recognition and cooperation cannot really exist without the sense of symbolism. This sense is now to a great extent corrupted and degenerate. Man cannot help making symbols of one sort or another; he is a being of symbols. But at present his symbols are not the product of spiritual creativity and vitality;

they are the symptoms of a violent illness, a technological cancer, from which he may not recover.

Meanwhile, the final answer does not remain entirely and exclusively in the hands of those who are still equipped to interpret ancient religious traditions. Nor is it in the hands of the scientist and technician. The artist and the poet seem to be the ones most aware of the disastrous situation, but they are for that very reason the closest to despair. If man is to recover his sanity and spiritual balance, there must be a renewal of communion between the traditional, contemplative disciplines and those of science, between the poet and the physicist, the priest and the depth psychologist, the monk and the politician.

Certainly the mere rejection of modern technology as an absolute and irremediable evil will not solve any problems. The harm done by technology is attributable more to its excessive and inordinately hasty development than to technology itself. It is possible that in the future a technological society *might* conceivably be a tranquil and contemplative one. In any case, it will do no good for us to remain specialists, enclosed in our respective fields, viewing with suspicion and disdain the efforts of others to make sense out of our world. We must try, together, to bring about a renewal of wisdom that must be more than a return to the past, however glorious. We need a wisdom appropriate to our own predicament: and such wisdom cannot help but begin in sorrow.

But one thing is certain, if the contemplative, the monk, the priest, and the poet merely forsake their vestiges of wisdom and join in the triumphant, empty-headed crowing of advertising men and engineers of opinion, then there is nothing left in store for us but total madness.

Cargo Cults of the South Pacific*

So-called Cargo Cults have emerged repeatedly, since colonial times, among the native populations of the South Sea
Islands and, in different forms, in Africa and Southeast
Asia. Messianic in nature, these cults vitally express the
deeply disturbed religious consciousness of the native faced
with a rapidly changing world. They represent his pathetic
and sometimes tragic effort to adjust to the culture foisted
upon him by white colonialism. Exotic, often bizarre systems
of ritualistic behavior, they might at first seem remote from
our own supposedly modern world. But it will be my contention that, rather than repudiating the Cargo Cults as
useless and misguided primitivism, we ought to ask ourselves if some of our own Western social and political movements are not, in fact, very similar to the Cargo Cults,
though perhaps less naïve. And we ought to ask if a sympathetic understanding of these cults might not tell us something important, not about the natives, but about ourselves.
But first it should be explained what Cargo Cults are.

* This is an edited version of a taped conference considerably
shortened for publication in *America*. The unedited transcription of the
conference is available at the Thomas Merton Studies Center, Bellarmine
College, Louisville, KY. —Ed.

For years after the coming of the white man, the islanders watched the activities of their white bosses and rulers and were disconcerted by the white man's powerful culture. They heard the white man talking about "kago" (pidgin for "cargo"). "Everything will be all right," the white man was saying, "when the kago comes. When the kago comes, we shall have pickles, and the cloth we need, and scissors, and the tobacco we are running out of. When the kago comes, we shall have beer and whiskey and rice."

Now many of these fabulous goods were things the native was not allowed to have. Hence, kago came to have a very important meaning for the native: the coming of a good time, when one would be like the whites and enjoy what the whites enjoyed—the coming of the millennium. It is important to see that the coming of kago was much more than a matter of obtaining wealth and enjoying the good life. It involved the crucially important question of the native's identity and of his relation to the white man. The difference between native and colonial was not merely one of color. It was the more radical distinction between those who could send for and receive cargo and those who never got any cargo of their own but depended on the white man for a rather miserable living.

For the native, then, to receive his own cargo would mean readmission to the human race. It would show him worthy of recognition as an equal to the white man. The problem was, therefore, one of identity, the native's place in the scheme of things, his human reality.

The native felt that something was being kept from him. The Bible that the Christian missionary had handed him seemed to have an important part missing, namely, the explanation of how one got cargo and became equal to the white man, how one achieved tangible and concrete evidence of brotherhood: a shared standard of living. To try to acquire this information, the native observed the white man busying himself with great fuss over the papers in his office. He saw the white man sitting on his porch and never, at least not in the native's terms, doing very much work. In fact, the white man did not seem to do a thing except strut around giving orders and signing papers, and then pretty soon a boat appeared, from across the sea, full of cargo.

The native tried to figure this out. What had the white man done to make this kago come? Since the native had never seen a factory or an industrial plant, and since the white man did not bother to make explanations, the native developed his own mythical explanation of how all this kago had come into being. It had been magically fashioned by the white man's dead ancestors from across the sea, with whom the white man had the secret of keeping in touch.

On the basis of his observation, the native evolved cults of symbolic activity, hoping to put himself in contact with the source of kago, thereby bringing about a situation in which kago would come for him and not just for the white man.

During the Yali movement, a Cargo Cult that arose in New Guinea around the middle of this century, someone got the idea that flowers played some part in the secret magic by which the whites obtained their cargo. It was observed that the white people liked to keep vases of fresh flowers in their dwellings, and that they would have flowers on the table when they gathered together for dinner. Thinking there might be some esoteric significance in this, the natives proceeded to decorate not only their houses but even whole villages with enormous amounts of flowers. Then, perhaps, kago might come to them as well.

In the Cargo movements in Melanesia, the natives destroyed their own wealth, not just the old kinds of native currency, but their own property, their own crops, their own livestock! The idea was that if you believed, you would destroy everything that was a link with the past. Destroy everything and then sit and wait. And in three days, five days, ten days, as a reward for this act of faith, kago will come to you and you will have all you sacrificed and everything else besides.

We are tempted, we Westerners, to regard such activity as a curious aberration, an irrational and crazed manifestation of a purely primitive mentality, the sort of ignorance we have long since left behind us. Such behavior, we think, is totally alien to us, simply another proof of our own superiority, the perfect justification of our attempts to keep the primitive peoples in tutelage and to subject them to our own political and economic way of life.

It would be a great mistake, however, to treat the participants in Cargo Cults as children, unable to take care of themselves and needing us to bring them reason, science, efficiency, and progress. A true understanding of the Cargo mentality can tell us much about ourselves.

We Westerners delude ourselves that we are utterly scientific and reasonable, that we have no myths. But this *is* one of our chief myths. We think we are objective, logical people, but we live imbedded in an enormous amount of mythology. And I would say that our Western mythology is not fundamentally different from, but only more complicated and sophisticated than, the mythology of the Cargo Cults.

We Westerners live surrounded by huge myths, which would seem, to a civilization more advanced than ours, as primitive and bizarre as the Cargo Cults' myths seem to us—but we do not realize it. Is there really much difference, though, between kago and the coming of the good life promised in our fabulous modern consumer advertising?

We Americans have to keep buying and consuming. The worst thing you can do here in America is to hold on to the past when the future is bursting in on you all the time in the form of new cars, new fashion designs, new houses, new styles of life. What was once satisfactory is now suddenly discovered to be inadequate, obsolete. There is an urgent need for new attitudes, a demand for a whole new view of things, a whole new way of doing things, because all of a sudden there is the feeling that things are getting away from you and that if you do not come up with new ideas fast, if you do not consume the new products fast, you are going to be left behind. The good life, the kago of modern America, will not come to you.

Common to all Cargo-type movements, then, is a need to abruptly repudiate everything old. This is what the Melanesians were doing when they destroyed their own worldly possessions. This is what is happening in modern China, where it is held that the only beliefs of value are those of Mao Tse-tung and young revolutionaries are constantly engaging in systematic attacks on everything old. This is what is happening here in America, where we imagine a sort of Grand Canyon between those older than twenty-six and those younger, whom we older folk imagine as ready to throw into the ocean everything that they receive from us. Likewise, in the American black-power movement, you have had a repudiation of non-violence and of Martin Luther King, Jr., a repudiation of the liberal, or moderate, normal political ways of settling things. Black power, in its extreme forms, seeks to discredit all compromise, all old ways of seeing and doing.

Either you accept the whole works, the whole Cargo message, or else you perish with the repudiated past. You are destroyed as irrelevant and obsolete. Take or leave it.

A Cargo movement need not necessarily be violent or aggressive. It can sometimes be quite peaceful, as in the case of the Indian Ghost Dance movement in America in the 1870's, where the idea was that if you danced for five days, washed in the river, and fulfilled other ritual prescriptions, then the dead would return, the old Indian manner of life be restored, the whites be driven out of the country. The important point is that common to all Cargo movements are just these sorts of ritual requirements, to be met with perfect exactitude. Sometimes it is dancing, sometimes fasting, sometimes carrying a gun—but the goal always is the destruction of something old as an act of faith in the future.

The final stage common to all Cargo Cults is, of course, their collapse. The Cargo prophet can work up a great deal of fervor with the idea that kago is coming right now or very soon. Naturally, this gets everybody terribly excited and delighted. But then, of course, the expectations are not met. The cargo does not come. People get disillusioned, or worse, destroyed. The Ghost Dance of the Indians, for instance, was stopped by a massacre by United States troops. Little has changed, at least in terms of the cult's initial expectations.

So the cult collapses. The faithful, having thoroughly committed themselves, having done all the things they were told to do, realize that it was useless, that the cargo is not coming. The cult collapses. And then it starts up again. Sooner or later it starts up again somewhere else nearby in a slightly different form. A year goes by, a couple of years go by, and there is a new prophecy. According to the English scholar, K. O. L. Burridge, in his book, *Mambu,* an excellent study of Cargo movements in New Guinea, the constant regeneration of Cargo activities indicates that there is something basically satisfying in the cult activities themselves, even when they do not get results. In other words, going through the motions of a Cargo Cult, going through the machinery of conversation and belief and commitment, making the sacrifices and abandoning the past, performing the ritual acts in preparation for the future and then sitting down and expecting the future, all this apparently reflects a very deep need in man. And if we could only sit back and open our eyes a little bit and realize what is going on, we would see the process everywhere. It is a basic myth-dream pattern common to everyone, including those who imagine themselves civilized.

Man wants to go through the Cargo Cult experience and does so repeatedly. Not only the natives of New Guinea, the Solomon Islands, the New Hebrides, and South Africa, but the blacks, the young Chinese, the white Westerners—everyone—all of us find the Cargo experience, in whatever form, vitally important. It is Burridge's idea, and I go along with it, that we need to be constantly readjusting, reshaping, putting together in new forms the basic symbols of our myth-dream. And it does not matter whether this myth-dream is totally naïve, totally legendary, or if it has a theological basis or a realistic political-scientific basis or whatever. It makes no difference. The deeper function of a Cargo Cult, then, is not to get cargo, but rather to bring a community together.

What about the activity we Catholics are going through now in our attempt at renewal? Doesn't it have some of the characteristics of a Cargo Cult? Isn't this a dreadful question? But I am not just asking it to be nasty. I think it would be really useful for us to consider, dispassionately and objectively, the possibility that we, too, are involved in the tidal wave of Cargo mentality, whether primitive or highly sophisticated, that is sweeping the world in all directions.

Myth is necessary and unavoidable. The unconscious has

a tremendous part to play in everything we do. It is part of our Western myth-dream to assume that everything we do has to be logical and scientific. But, under the cover of being logical, we sometimes permit ourselves to be very illogical indeed.

Consider the Vietnam war. We saw ourselves there as a big brother helping a little brother. But who is our brother? The little Vietnamese brother we are trying to help may suddenly turn out to be a Communist brother, whom we do not regard as a brother at all but as a devil. And this suddenly overwhelms any element of brotherliness in our rather deluded dream about our relation with the Vietnamese. And what about our Catholic myth-dream? Isn't it clear only in theory and ambivalent in practice? There are undoubtedly some strange and complex elements in a dream that justifies killing out of love.

What are we to make of such inconsistency? It may be that the myth material of the Cargo Cults, which we tend to discard as bizarre, irrelevant, and arbitrary, has a fundamental truth to reveal to us, from which we can profit if only we can decode it and apply its message, which we have so long failed to see, to our own misguided lives.

Exploring the myth of the two brothers (part of a Cargo Cult that emerged not so long ago in New Guinea), Mr. Burridge takes us really out of our depths as white people. The two brothers became separated, due to an accidental act by one brother, who killed a certain kind of fish and, in so doing, violated a taboo. As a result, the brothers were separated by an ocean. One of them, the one who killed the fish, remained at a disadvantage. He was no longer intelligent or successful, as was the other. He remained on the level of primitive culture, while his brother advanced, acquiring all kinds of new knowledge and goods.

This myth is trying to explain the difference between the

Kanaka (the New Guinean) and the white man. And the message boils down to this: all men are brothers and that some men are better off than others by virtue of their having greater gifts and skills does not mean that they are essentially better. It simply means that they have quite by chance avoided mistakes and stumbled onto lucky answers. It might well have happened the other way around. The native of New Guinea might well have had the right answers and progressed first. Some men are more fortunate than others, but not superior. They are still all brothers.

As the native grapples with his "inferiority" and with the sense of guilt instilled in him by the superior endowment and prosperity of the white man, he arrives at a basic truth. He tells himself: "Look. You do not have to feel guilty because you are black. It does not mean you are worse. You do not have to feel guilty because the white man has cargo and you do not. This is not a sign that you are bad. It is not a sign that you are helpless. You can, and should, have cargo, too."

Now this is an extraordinary thing, because this is also the meaning of the black-power movement in America; only the black-power movement is not spelling it out in a bizarre primitive myth. But black people everywhere are in this tremendous identity crisis, struggling with a feeling of guilt about being black and trying to arrive at a real conviction that being black does not mean being worse. In black power, as in Cargo, the black is seeking to establish his identity as one capable of getting equality by himself, rather than waiting to receive it as a benevolent gift from the white man, and on the white man's terms.

The white man never manages to understand this. He fails completely to get any such message out of Cargo Cults. On the contrary, his response is one of fear and incomprehension.

He feels that some eerie kind of magic is being used against him, just as most unintelligent American whites felt that Martin Luther King's non-violence movement was somehow a threat and an attack on them.

It seems to me so terribly important that we learn to read into these Cargo movements what is really there, and thus help to deliver ourselves from this awful superstition of white superiority. But, instead, we feel we have the only answer, and of course we are willing to help our black brother, but the help is offered in arrogant, vain, self-complacent terms. We will only help him to be exactly like us, while at the same time making it impossible for him to be like us. So we put him in an impossible bind and then wonder why he feels anguished.

All non-white people, all the underprivileged people of the world, seem to feel an enormous yearning for authentic reciprocity with the white man, symbolized by eating together, sitting down at a table together, accepting one another as sharers of the same food. Jesus raised this great human gesture to high religious dignity in the Eucharist. But how often this great sign of brotherhood, the Eucharist, has been robbed of its meaning. How often it has meant anything but what it is supposed to mean, which is that rich and poor, white and native, sit down and eat together. The white colonial and the native never sat down to an actual meal in the home. If the white man wanted to share his food with the native, he sent a can of corned beef out the back door and said: "Here, eat it." He threw it to the native as to a dog. There was no moral reciprocity at all.

The disturbing truth begins to come clear. Our white myth-dream *demands* reciprocity with non-white people, because it takes as its axiom our total superiority over everybody else! Like the South Sea native, we, too, have a myth-

dream, but ours is profoundly un-Christian and even profoundly inhuman. Even when we do manage to treat the
non-white peoples as humans, we still treat them as *inferior*
humans. Even when we think we are being nice and fair and
just, we are living and acting out a dream that makes fair-
ness and justice impossible. Even when we are being kind
and liberal, our kindness and liberality are tinged with unconscious racism. Black power, among other things, is trying
to tell us so.

Our myth-dream is tied up in self-admiration over the
fact that we know how to make money. We have this secret,
the secret of cargo, which our inferiors do not have. Of
course, we pretend that we want to share our secret with
everybody. We want to bring everybody else into the same
affluence that we have. But we do not mean what we say.
We want to use our inferiors for our own profit. We invest
in them in such a way that the underdeveloped countries
are maintained in subjection to us. Our myth-dream main-
tains itself by putting everybody else into an economic and
cultural bind in respect to ourselves.

Then, when the native or black tries to get out of this
bind, our inability to understand his mentality results in the
mobilization, on our part, of a racist counter-myth. The
function of this counter-myth is the repudiation of the native
as a person, the discrediting of the native in his drive for
identity. We refuse to accept his drive for identity because
it does not fit in with our own myth-dream. For example,
what sane businessman would pay attention for two seconds
to the myth of the Kanaka Mambu, a hero-figure in one of
the New Guinea Cargo Cults, who went to Australia and
came back with the secret of cargo, claiming he could now
produce money literally out of thin air? It is just sheer
nonsense as far as we are concerned. Blinded by our own
myth-dream, we become oppressive, despotic, and, finally,

murderous in our need to discredit the threatening myth-dream of the native.

Consider the outcome of the Yali movement's attempt to use flowers as a magical symbol. When the natives, thinking the flowers the colonialists kept on their dining-room tables held the secret of cargo, decorated their own homes and even entire villages with flowers, the Europeans began to get touchy. Any signs of flowers in a native house or of floral decorations in the villages were regarded with great suspicion. Soon the police began taking flowers away from the natives and destroying them, even searching the natives' houses for hidden flowers.

But this merely confirmed the natives in their belief that the Europeans had some secret which they were withholding from the Kanakas, and that this secret had to do with flowers. Otherwise, why should the Europeans go to such lengths to destroy bouquets in the native houses? While the Kanakas were operating consciously within a myth, the Europeans, thinking that they, the Europeans, had no myth, were unconsciously responding to the native myth, driven on by the white-supremacy myth-dream of their own. Such a little incident as the natives' use of flowers, in itself natural and innocent and healthy, came to be interpreted as a suspicious and threatening manifestation of anti-white revolt. Suspiciousness of this sort soon becomes a self-fulfilling prophecy, engendering the very kind of repression that will provoke revolt.

The myth-dream of absolute white supremacy brooks no opposition. We need to guard jealously and preserve our white myth-dream, even though it is not, as we have seen, fundamentally different from the Cargo mentality. It is our collective daydream, made up of all kinds of common symbols and beliefs with which we are collectively at ease. We readily exchange these elements among ourselves, pass them around in conversation and especially through the mass media. When a myth-dream is constantly in the papers and on TV, it seems pretty real!

So we create this great common fund of ideas, attitudes, jokes, nicknames, brand names, stereotyped needs for certain products, standard reactions toward events—and it all goes together to make up the stuff of our actual life. The content of our conscious and unconscious minds is largely drawn from this common myth-dream. It is the basis on which we interpret our whole existence and on which we rest our most vital decisions. And when we imagine it to be threatened, we often create, in our paranoia, the very opposition we fear. We *need* opposition and rebellion in order to act out our fears and hostilities by suppressing those we imagine to be threatening us. U.S. troops ended the Indian Ghost Dance with a massacre. The anti-guerrilla forces in Bolivia, supported by the C.I.A., killed Che Guevara and transformed him into a martyred hero of mythic proportions all over the world.

In Vietnam, with all our immense technological skill, with all the tremendous versatility of the destructive weapons that we have devised, the struggle takes on mythical dimensions of an absolutely disastrous nature for the United States, if seen, as the Third World sees it, as a struggle between a small minority of poorly armed but dedicated guerrillas against the enormous technological might of the richest country in the world. We throw in billions of dollars' worth of all kinds of weapons, and the net result is a Third World myth-dream of resistance fighters asserting their identity and dignity. For the United States, even if it wins, this is simply fatal.

And so, in our blindness, we are providing the non-white peoples with the essentially needed mythical elements to build up this vital myth-dream of theirs. We are giving them confidence and a sense of identity. More and more, they are becoming aware that they can oppose white power and white technological might with their naked human dignity, and not only survive but win at least a moral victory. One can only lament the tragic inability of the American public to grasp this aspect of the struggle, an inability born of the same jealous need to guard our white myth-dream that prevents us from reading the real message of the Cargo Cults.

If only we could understand the moral principles at work in the Cargo Cult myth-dreams and translate them into political action, the Cargo Cults would die out. They would no longer be needed. But we are prevented from doing so by our tendency to see Cargo Cults as anti-white rather than pro-native.

To quote Mr. Burridge: "One cannot but feel that Europeans who see in the Cargo Cults little more than reaction to white domination are taking themselves more seriously than do Kanakas. For Kanakas, the problem is more urgent and more personal than whether they shall be ruled by white men. They want to know where they stand in the world as men."

The point of this study has not been to discover something curious and exotic but to reach the heart of our own problem, the universal problem of communication. Our communication with primitives and primitive societies demands that we first communicate with something deep in ourselves, something with which we are out of touch. It is our own primitive self, which has become alienated, hostile, and strange.

The white man interprets the Cargo myth either as greed or as naïve error about the processes of manufacture and distribution, and in so doing, he interprets it (or misinterprets it) in his own favor. He ignores the real message of the Cargo myth, which is the demand that the white man meet all peoples on a basis of moral equality and reciprocity.

The white man's myth-dream impels him, even when he is trying, with supposed disinterest, to help the native, to act in such a way as to ensure the native's moral surrender and submission.

Quoting Burridge again: "Neither missionary nor administrative officer demands a quid pro quo in the economic field. On the contrary, each personally, as well as in a representative capacity, provides Kanakas with cash, the opportunity to earn cash and with material goods. Neither asks for a like return, but each does demand the Kanaka's moral surrender and acquiescence to a highly variegated and systematized set of political and religious forms and beliefs. In effect, this is playing Mephistopheles, attempting to buy a man's soul."

If our white Western myth-dream demands of us that we spiritually enslave others in order to "save" them, we should not be surprised when their own myth-dream demands of them that they get entirely free of us to save themselves. But both the white man's and the native's myth-dreams are only partial and inadequate expressions of the whole truth. It is not that the primitive needs to be dominated by the white man in order to become fully human. Nor is it that he needs to get rid of the white man. Each needs the other, to cooperate in the common enterprise of building a world adequate for the historical maturity of man.

II
SEVEN WORDS

FOR NED O'GORMAN

I Death

"Death is the end of life."

This statement seems at first sight quite obvious. It appears to say everything essential about death. Yet merely to declare that when a living being ceases to live, it "dies," is perhaps to say nothing of any importance at all. If we reflect on the implications of "life" and "death" and the "end of life," we become uneasily aware that to make purely casual statements about these realities—a statement which turns out to say "nothing of importance"—is a frivolous abuse of speech. This reveals an incapacity to face the reality of life, death, and the end of life. Death is treated with frivolity because life itself is treated with frivolity.

Life comes into being without any invitation of our own: we suddenly find ourselves in it. And as soon as we recognize ourselves as alive we become aware that we tend toward inevitable death. If we do not gain some adequate understanding of our life and our death, during the life-span that is ours, our life will become nothing but a querulous refusal, a series of complaints that it must end in death. Then the fear of death becomes so powerful that it results in a flat refusal of life. Life itself becomes a negation, a neurosis, a frivolity.

When life and death lose their proper meaning, that is to say, when they are no longer experienced as what they really are, then the awful and empty power of death creeps into everything and sickens everything. So when death becomes most trivial, it also becomes most pervasive. It is only "the end of life." So all life ends. All is death. Why live?

To take death seriously is not, by any means, to seek to avoid it always and at all costs, but to see that it must come as part of a development, as part of a living continuity that has an inner meaning of its own. Death contributes something decisive to the meaning of life. Therefore, death does not simply "intervene" or "supervene" and spring upon life as upon its prey, in order to devour it. To hypostatize death, to give it an objective and autonomous reality of its own, a "power" of its own, and set it over against life, makes death not serious but trivial. And yet this way of thinking does, in fact, give death a kind of power over life, at least in our own minds. Thus, we *live as if* death were always ready to exercise this inescapable power over us. We take to living mouse lives that are always waiting for the cat, death. Yet there is no cat, and we are not mice. If we do, in fact, "die," it is not because a monster has caught up with us and pounced on us at last. If we become obsessed with the idea of death hiding and waiting for us in ambush, we are not making death more real but life less real. Our life is divided against itself. It becomes a tug of war between the love and the fear of itself. Death then operates in the midst of life, not the end of life, but rather, as the *fear* of life. Death is life afraid to love and trust itself because it is obsessed with its own contingency and its own ending.

That we inevitably take this wrong attitude toward life and death (we cannot help it) is, according to the Bible, the sign and the effect of sin. Sin and death go together, for when our attitude toward life becomes infected with sin (and every man's attitude is so infected), then life is seen as something that must inevitably be ambushed by death. But when is life seen in such a light? This is the important question, for on this depends our notion of the *end* of life. And when we pause to reconsider this fact, we see that the word "end" is ambiguous. This ambiguity is close to the heart of that ignorance of life (and consequent fear of death) which is, in its turn, such an important element in what we call "sin."

The *"end"*: that is to say, the *termination, abrupt and arbitrary conclusion*. The Greeks thought of the thread of life being cut off by the scissors of the Fates. Death is, then, the destruction of something that need not end. The termination of the interminable. This brings us to a better idea of the sinful concept of life: the word "interminable" is quite suggestive. Though there is no real reason why life should simply go on and on and on, we feel that this interminability is nevertheless due to life. We find that life is, therefore, an incomprehensible *datum,* something thrust upon us, something that wants to continue, something that even though meaningless declares itself, in its inmost strivings and aspirations, to be "interminable." This experience of life which we are now characterizing as that which is born of sin, is therefore completely ambiguous and, in fact, very distressing. Life is something meaningless that seeks to perpetuate itself without reason and to be simply and arbitrarily interminable. Over against this is death, which is life's enemy, and seeks, always with ultimate success, to terminate it. Two arbitrary forces meet in this unreasonable conflict and death always wins. Something which for no reason wants to be interminable is, in fact, terminated. An essentially meaningless life-drive demands to continue in spite of everything, and we choose to adjust our lives to this demand. But the situation itself seems fatally unjust. Therefore, we tend, as sinners, to meet it equivocally. We know that death cannot be turned aside by deceit, yet nevertheless we try to live lives that will at least outwit death as long as possible. The sinful life is one which for no reason, except that we seek to outwit death, becomes a hectic and desperate drive to assert life's own interminability. This compounds all the inner ambiguities of life and death. For one thing, in seeking to convince themselves of their own power to survive, men seek to destroy others who are weaker than themselves. In destroying others, the victors strive to feel themselves interminable, since in the presence of another's suffering and death they themselves go on more

lustily than before. They go home and celebrate their new
lease on life—which has, however, come from the experience and spectacle of death. In the society of men who are
exclusively intent on their own pleasure and survival, even
though it has no meaning, just because they are convinced
that their life ought to be interminable, death begins to
play a very important part. Death is called upon to nourish
and to stimulate the "sense of life."

This immediately begets another and far worse ambiguity.
A "sense of life" that is habitually fed on death is corrupt
and pathological. It is not life at all. In seeking to escape
death, man becomes fatally attracted by the death he seeks
to escape. His obsession with avoiding death becomes a fas-
cinated and hypnotized flirtation with death. Thus, death
in fact comes to be the "end" of life, not in the sense of its
termination only, but more especially as its *goal*.

Psychoanalysis has taught us something about the death
wish that pervades the modern world. We discover our affluent society to be profoundly addicted to the love of death,
and most of all when it seems to be carried away by the
celebration of life. Erich Fromm has pointed out how obsession with power and wealth inevitably means obsession with
death. The death-oriented mind not only directs its energies
to obviously destructive uses of power (such as nuclear stock-
piling) but even its apparently productive work is, in fact,
a work of death, a work centered on reducing life to "dead
things" and depersonalizing men, reducing them to objects,
to commodities for use. The love of money is, in fact, the love
of a "dead" product (which is nevertheless endowed with
magic life), and we know how psychoanalysis explains this.
The anal character is a death-loving character, and he expresses his love of death not only in avarice, in the accumulation of power, but also in legalism (the deadening of life
and impulse by the hand of law), technologism (the substi-

tution of mechanical order for the fertile unpredictability of life), as well as by the direct cult of violence for its own sake.

Thus, we see that in a death-oriented society, even though it may seem very dynamic and powerful, *death becomes the end of life in the sense of its goal,* and this is made at least symbolically evident by the fact that money, machines, bombs, etc., are all regarded as more important than living people. In such a society, though much may officially be said about human values, whenever there is, in fact, a choice between the living and the dead, between men and money, or men and power, or men and bombs, then the choice will always be for death, *for death is the end or the goal of life.*

Nevertheless, this idea of death as goal, fruit, or fulfillment is not completely false or misleading, once the context of sin is understood and accepted. But now death as "end" must be seen in a totally different light—the light not of sin and selfishness but of love and grace.

All created life is limited. Living beings come into existence and begin at once to develop, for growth is one of the essential functions of life. In the beginning of its growth, the living being must continually receive from others. The human infant, totally helpless and dependent on its parents, shows this clearly enough. In this state of vulnerability and limitation, the human heart already faces the problem of death, and it is here that infantile man, whose very nature it is to regard himself as interminable, as one for whom others have to live and sacrifice themselves, forms his cunning idea of death. But man's ideas must grow as he grows. The infantile concept of survival at any cost is a kind of absolute. It must be outgrown. As man grows into other stages of human development, he realizes that there are ways in which *life affirms itself by consenting to end.* For example, the youth begins to discover that by bringing to an end some egoistic satisfaction, in order to do something for another, he can discover a deeper level of reality and of life. The mature man realizes that his life affirms itself most, not in acquiring things for himself, but in giving his time, his efforts, his strength, his intelligence, and his love to others. Here a different kind of dialectic of life and death begins to appear. The living drive, the vital satisfaction, by "ending" its trend to self-satisfaction and redirecting itself to and for others, transcends itself. It "dies" insofar as the ego is concerned, for the self is deprived of immediate satisfactions which it could once claim without being contested. Now it renounces these things, in order to give to others. Hence, life "dies" to itself in order to give itself away, and thus affirms itself more maturely, more fruitfully, and more completely. We live in order to die to ourselves and give everything to others. This concept of "dying" is, in fact, altogether different from the death-loving attitude we have sketched above, for, in point of fact, this is not death-loving or death-centered at all. The "dying" to self in order to give to others is nothing more or less than a higher and more special affirmation of life. Such dying is the fruit of life, the evidence of mature and productive living. It is, in fact, the end or the goal of life.

But since contingent lives must end—they are not interminable and there is nothing whatever in their constitution that justifies us in thinking that they are—it is important that the end of life itself should finally set the seal upon the giving and the sacrifice which has marked mature and productive living. Thus, man physically and mentally declines, having given everything that he had to life, to other men, to his love, to his family, and to his world. He is spent or exhausted, not in the sense that he is merely burned out and gutted by the accumulation of money and power, but because he has given himself totally in love. There is nothing left now for him to give. It is now that in a final act he surrenders his life itself.

This is "the end of life," not in the sense of a termination, but in the sense of a *culminating gift*, the last free perfect act of love which is at once surrender and acceptance: the surrender of his being into the hands of God, who made it, and the acceptance of the death which in its details and circumstances is perhaps very significantly in continuity with all the acts and incidents of life—its good and its bad, its sins and its love, its conquests and its defeats. Man's last gift of himself in death is, then, the acceptance of what he has been and the resignation of all final judgment as to the meaning of his life, its worth, its point, its ultimate destiny. It is the final seal his freedom sets upon the love and the trust with which it has striven to live.

For a Christian, this sublimation of death by freedom and love can only be the result of a free gift of God in which our personal death is united with the mystery of Christ's death on the Cross. The death of Christ is not simply the juridical payment of an incomprehensible ransom which somehow makes us acceptable at the gate of heaven. It has radically transformed the sinful death of man into a liberating and victorious death, a supreme act of faith and love, because it also transforms man's life by faith and love. The obedience of Christ transforms the death of man into an act of glad acceptance and of love which transcends death and carries him over into eternal life with the Risen Christ.

It is, of course, understood that, for Christian theology, death "in Christ" is not merely a matter of external forms but of interior grace, and this grace can be and is given to every man, Christian or not, whose death is, in fact, the last free culminating gift in a fruitful life oriented to ultimate truth in God (whether known or unknown, but at least implicitly loved and sought).

Without the Cross of Christ, His love, freedom, and grace,

death grinds down upon the last despairing spark of life and triumphs over it, because the spark, still clinging to its own illusion of interminability, refuses to give itself back to that from which it came. Hence, various religious illustrations of this defeat: for Hinduism and Buddhism, the man who clings to interminability must in fact go on being born over and over again, since that is what he does in fact want. In the Christian tradition, this "interminable" loveless and meaning-less existence is called hell. (We must, of course, remember that the graphic descriptions of hell's torments are more or less literary and are not expected to be taken literally just as they stand. Sartre's idea of hell in *No Exit* is, in fact, much closer to Christian theology than are the lurid pictures of devils with pitchforks pitching sinners into the hottest flame.)

The life of heaven, eternal life in Christ, is not simply a life without end. It is not interminable joy—even joy, if *interminable,* would become dreadful. The suggestive word "inter-minable" contains a hint that something that would be better terminated cannot, in fact, be put to an end. It never ceases! It goes on forever. Who would want a joy that he could never get rid of? Eternal life, on the other hand, has nothing in it which would be better if it were ended. The very concept of an end is no longer relevant, for the goal is attained. There is, then, no more goal, there is no end. All is present and all is actual. All is *pure reality,* the total compact fulfillment of man in love and in vision, not measured out in infinitely extended time, but grounded in the depths of the personal life of God and the inner dynamic of love: from the abyss of the Father, in the light of the Son, through the love of the Holy Spirit.

Death is the point at which life, by freely and totally giv-ing itself, enters into this ground and this infinite act of love. Death is the point at which life can, if we so choose, become perfectly real, not because it "demands to be interminable," but because it can receive the gift of pure actuality in the love of God, in the Trinitarian life, the circumincession of Persons. Death is, then, the point at which life can attain its pure fulfillment. Death brings life to its goal. But the goal is not death—the goal is perfect life.

II Theology

Theology is the act of the believing person reflecting upon his belief and studying it methodically in order to reach a deeper understanding of God's revelation and to surrender himself more fully and more intelligently to God's manifest will and plan of salvation in the contemporary world.

The classic expression of the task of theology is the saying of St. Augustine inspired by a line of the Septuagint and taken up by St. Anselm and the whole medieval tradition: *credo ut intelligam,* I believe in order to understand. Theology is the intelligence of God that is the fruit of loving, inquiring, and investigating faith. The tasks of faith and of theology need to be seen in their distinctness. By faith the person receives God's word and assents to it because it is His word. By faith the person "hears" God (Romans 10:17). That is to say, he not only hears *about* God but enters into a personal relationship of obedient love with God his Father, who is offering him the message of salvation in and through the Church, the faithful and redeemed community. Theology in the true sense starts not merely with certain formal authoritative propositions about God but from this personal relationship. The task of theology is not merely to improve our scientific understanding of dogmas but to deepen and enlighten our personal relationship with God in the Church.

It is clear from this that theology must not be regarded statically as a "package" which one acquires, possesses, and makes use of. It is a job, an active work not only of the theological intelligence but also of the whole person. This means that theology is not simply concerned with establishing that such and such a proposition is revealed by God and is a truth of faith. It also discovers the import of revealed truth for man in terms of his human and earthly life in all its dimensions. Theology is, therefore, not merely an esoteric study of what is considered strictly supernatural as opposed to everything in the realm of nature and matter and apart from it. On the contrary, theology sees the entire world of nature and matter, and all the human concerns of man and his society in their relation to the plan of God's love for the ultimate fulfillment and perfection of man and the world in Christ. Hence, every branch of human science and art may turn out to be relevant for theology, and a theology which presumes at the same time to judge human disciplines and to ignore them is hardly fulfilling its proper task. We need not pause here to examine the irrelevancies and confusions that have arisen from a conflict between science and theology that has been notorious for nothing so much as for semantic chaos.

Theology, as we have said, is grounded in a personal relationship of enlightened faith in which the believer, as a member of the faithful community, is taught by the revelation of Christ, the "author and finisher of faith" (Hebrews 12:2). In this dimension of personal relationship with a revealing and illuminating God, theology is seen not only as science but also as wisdom, not only as study and method, but also as contemplation and love. Thus, Evagrius Ponticus could say (fourth century), the true theologian is the man of prayer. But this must not lead us to underestimate or to obscure the central importance of the intelligence and of methodical judgment in theology. Theology is not merely a diffuse and religious appreciation of revealed truth but a scientific study aimed at acquiring strict certitudes. These certitudes, in turn, are necessary to deepen and strengthen the fidelity of the Church and the clear-sighted obedience of the faithful to God's salvific will. In an era of revolutionary change, one of the crucially important tasks of theology will be the clarification of this fidelity and obedience in terms of the actual human condition and the current world view of secular man in his secularity. A theology which is completely out of touch with the human problems of our age, which encloses itself in the categories of a world view that no longer speaks with any relevance to modern man, and demands "obedience" to a static and purely juridical order that serves reaction and the status quo rather than crying human needs, both material and spiritual, is no longer fulfilling its function, because it is obscuring that area where the will of God seeks most insistently to manifest itself to us. The theology of each age is necessarily a debtor to the human needs of that age, because Christian theology is the elucidation of a salvific message addressed to all men in the context of their own time and their own history. The task of theology is not only to give the Church an accurate understanding of "timeless" truths but, much more, to point out how she may exercise her mission to serve man in his most pressing and authentic needs, in their actual existential reality here and now. In an age when man is crushed under unreasonable and unjust social structures and menaced with the threat of destruction in a ruthless power struggle which ignores all his true interests, it is evident that the most radical changes are called for in the most urgent way. The only theological outlook adequate for our time is one which is frankly and unashamedly open to the need for revolutionary change in man's secular world. A detached, academic, purely speculative consideration of essences and attributes, a contemplation of formalities and an exquisite examination of purely spiritual causalities will no longer serve as theology in this century.

III Divine

Perhaps no word could be more difficult to talk about intelligently than this one. Can God be approached through an adjective? Inevitably, the use of an adjective, "divine," suggests a special quality of God. But as in God there are no qualities, we can understand at once that, in fact, the term divine is most often used in reference to some created participation in the life of God. For instance, one can contemplate the "divine light," or one can be illuminated by "divine faith" (in these cases the term "divine" refers to God as the *source* of light and the *authority* upon whose word one must believe). We live the "divine life" of "divine sonship" by "divine grace," because the "divine image" is restored in us by the action of the in-dwelling Holy Spirit. In all these examples the word "divine" refers not to God's own Being and Essence but to a participated-in and Godlike quality in man. The word "divine" is most properly used to refer not to substance but to accident, not to God Himself but to a created participation in His life. However, we do, of course, find many expressions like the "divine essence," "divine goodness," etc., which do not always belong to the best tradition in theology. Yet it must be admitted that even in the Bible we find the adjective "divine" used—in a rare and exceptional case. In the Second Epistle of St. Peter (1:4) the life of grace is described as a "participation in the divine nature."

"Divine grace" is, then, the gift of godlikeness in a creature who is loved by God as His son. "Divine sonship" is the quality of a creature that has entered into a special relationship with God. This relationship is a "divine life" activated by "divine love."

What is it that makes a man's life "divine"? Surely if this special quality characterizes him, it must in some sense be recognizable. The "divine" life is, in fact, characterized by a faith which frees man from all forms of servitude, even and perhaps especially in religious matters (see Galatians *passim*). This faith brings him under the direct guidance of the Holy Spirit of love living in the Church of God. The "divine" man, or the "son of God," is then, paradoxically, marked by a great humility and self-effacement. He is not violent but forgiving and kind (Matthew 5:43–48). He is free from any need for aggressive self-assertion. He does not worry about his own needs, but trusts completely in God for everything (Matthew 6:19–34). The man who leads a "divine" life is, then, a perfect son of God in imitation of Christ, who in all things looked only to the will and love of His Father. The divine man lives in constant contact with an inner source of divine life, or as Meister Eckhart would have said, "the divine birth within us." Let us quote Eckhart on godlikeness:

Who are they that are like God? . . . There is nothing like the divine being for in him there is neither idea nor form. Therefore those sons that are like God are the ones to whom God has given himself evenly withholding nothing. All the Father can give he gives to them evenly . . . when they do not consider themselves to be more than others and are no more dear to themselves than others are.

In such typical expressions the word "divine" points to an origin in God or a finality in God or some likeness to God. But if we examine more closely, we find that when the word "divine" is used even of these created entities, it is more a refusal to explain than an actual explanation.

To say that something is human is to make it quite explicit and to reveal characteristics that we can quite clearly know because, being men, we know and experience in ourselves the things that are proper to man. To say, on the other hand, that something is divine is to say that we do not quite know what it is, in fact, that we cannot penetrate its meaning perfectly, and what we know about it is drawn from a mysterious "divine revelation," that is to say, it is made known in messages and words that have come from God. But who or what is God?

To say that God is simply the "divine Being" might lead to a total misunderstanding, if it indicated that among all the beings that can be there is one who is superior to the others, and this one is called "divine." As though God differed specifically from other beings by his "divinity," just as man differs specifically from other beings by his humanity. Can such statements make real sense? It is no news to anyone that the "God of the philosophers" whom Pascal rejected in turning to the "God of Abraham, Isaac and Jacob" (who appeared to him as living fire), the deist God who is a mere celestial watchmaker or a "supreme Being," has long since ceased to have much meaning in the world, which can get along perfectly well without any such hypothesis. That is one of the things most wrong with the word "divine" as applied to God Himself, rather than to creatures who share in His mysterious life. To call God a "divine being" may well, in certain contexts, merely postulate Him as a hypothesis and, therefore, automatically suggest that He is a being no longer seriously discussed in polite society. Hence, we may say that the God of the Bible is not revealed as "divine being" for whom there is a convenient classification. The Old Testament has several names for God, all of which are proper names and all of which oppose Him to the "divinities" or Baalim to which idols can be erected. This almost suggests that the term "divine" is fated to become implicitly idolatrous unless it is treated with extreme care. A concept can quite easily become idolatrous when it is abstract (as "divine" is) and the temptation to make idols of seemingly scientific abstractions is much greater to modern man than it was to the ancients.

The great self-revelation of Yahweh to Moses (Exodus

3:14) is at once completely concrete and perfectly transcendent. "I am who am," or "I am He who is," or "I am who I
am," or again, "I am He who sends you"—these various mysterious possibilities which are not even "names" in a strict
sense do not reveal a "divine nature" with distinct properties,
though in a certain theological context one can reason from
this revelation to a system of propositions about the divine
nature and aseity (by-him-selfness) as pure actuality, absolute
Being.

The manifestation of the "divine" is, therefore, not a manifestation of any special quality but of radical being, actuality,
aliveness, power, love, concern. And all this is manifested
historically by the deeds that flow from the commands and
missions of the hidden One, who simply "is."

What is, therefore, important about the Biblical theology
of God is not the explication of a "divine nature" but of God's
acts in the world. These acts are "great works" (*magnalia*),
but not always necessarily marked by a special extraordinary
"divine" character. On the contrary, the scandal of the Old
Testament—Genesis, for instance—is to some modern readers
the fact that so many of God's acts are perfectly ordinary and
seemingly trivial: the choice of a wife for Isaac, or the skill with
which Jacob becomes rich. These are hardly what we would
call "divine" acts in the sense of having a special and mar-
velous character about them. But they are nevertheless the
acts of God. Hence, there is a disconcerting aura of secularity
about much of God's activity as recorded in the Bible, and
uneasiness with this has generally led certain types of philo-
sophic religiosity to improve on the concept of God, seeking to
make it more spiritual, more impressive to man's mind, in a
word, more "divine."

In dealing with the word "divine," therefore, we must be
careful to discern whether it is being bestowed on God by the
graciousness of some philosopher or whether it really repre-

sents something that has been made known in the baffling ordinariness of "divine revelation."

IV Purity

"Father, I have sinned against purity."

The frequent use of this discreet and decorous cliché in the confessional has eventually brought the word "purity" into a kind of discredit from which no intervention of ours, however zealous, can rescue it today. It remains only for us to see what the expression may signify, to consider the misunderstandings that can arise from it, and to suggest that there are, after all, other possible meanings to be remembered. But first let us begin with the "sin against purity." Is the very concept of a "sin against purity" perhaps itself a sin against purity? Does it convey an implicit falsification of certain important aspects of human nature? Does it make the whole question of sex impossibly confusing?

Let us inquire into what is meant here by "pure" and "impure." We are at once confronted with a grave semantic misfortune. A refinement of juridical hairsplitting (fortunately unknown to most penitents) has reduced the concept of purity to a very elusive and complex one. The erection that occurs spontaneously without forethought is not impure, or at any rate is "less impure" than one which is deliberately induced by looking at a picture of the Queen of Burlesque, but this, on the other hand, suddenly becomes less impure, or indeed pure, if the looker is a moral theologian hunting down an interesting case in the line of duty. In the long run, whether you are pure or not seems to depend on who your lawyer is.

In any event, the concept of purity tends to be compounded of two elements. The pure is the asexual and the anaesthetic. Man is "pure" when he either has no sexual reactions at all, or when he does not enjoy them, or when he would rather not have them, or when he has done his best to make them hateful and frustrating, or when they are strictly in the line of duty (marital intercourse). To have a slight velleity for sexual pleasure is a bit impure. To get an erection is more so. To touch sexual organs—one's own or those of others—is still more so. To have an orgasm is most so. This whole attitude of abstraction, of hatred and denigration of the body, has finally led to a pathological and totally unrealistic obsession with bodily detail. The custom of penitential tariffs, which goes back to the Irish monastic codes of the High Middle Ages, has, so to speak, "priced" the various acts and parts of the body with appropriate penalties, and this has resulted in a dreadful atomization of love. One could go on at length to develop this idea—not confined to religion by any means —in which love puts the human body on the market, either as a desirable package of commodities and pleasures or as a highly dangerous compound of moral evils. Love becomes no longer an expression of the communion between persons but a smorgasbord of the senses in which one selects what he wants—or what he thinks he can get away with. Unfortunately, this creates a very special kind of mentality which enables certain persons to manage an aborted sex life as follows: when you have sexual velleities mentally, you cancel them out by saying you don't want them (but you go on having them). As to the rest, just be careful that if they happen they are always accidents, and in order to reassure yourself on this point, make certain that they always take place in some manner that is extremely frustrating, humiliating, and unpleasant, or at least inconvenient, so you can be sure you did not "want" them with full deliberation—nobody in his right mind would. Yet do not ask the question: Are you in your right mind? Let it suffice that you have "preserved your purity."

Would it be too much to recommend a revision of the notion of purity that would also enable people to stay fully human?

It will readily be seen that this decadent concept of purity, which has lost all Christian character whatever, depends on a certain stereotyped view of man and of the world. It would be unfair to distinguish this view by calling it Neoplatonic, for it is only the exhausted remnant of a once living and sophisticated world view. But, in any event, the typical style it takes is one in which matter is discredited; sense, passion, and emotion are feared and detested; purity is associated with spirit or perhaps more crudely with the "mental" and the "intentional" or the "volitive." A dash of pseudostoicism will make this a totally voluntaristic exercise. One crushes sense with an act of will. Add a little Jansenism and Manichaeism and you can concoct a gruesome dose of self-hate and loathing for the flesh. This can also combine with a lusty fascination with all forms of "impurity," and even a regular cult of sin, which, of course, takes the righteous form of sin hunting, censoriousness, planting fig leaves on statues, and banning obscene movies—of which there are doubtless more than enough. After all, the manias of the pure have contributed to the development of a very special kind of impurity, the salaciousness that always goes as far as a code permits, while suggesting all that an average vulgar imagination can conjure up without effort.

What must frankly be said about this perverse conception of purity is that in reality it does nothing at all to bring sexual desire under the control of a free and mature intelligence, in service of the highest good of human persons. On the contrary, a morbid, unreasonable, and prurient approach to sex only degrades and perverts the sexual instinct leading it into forms of expression which, in their sado-masochism and hypocritical selfishness, are far more dangerous, much more radically "impure" than the normal expression of erotic love. This pessimistic and negative concept of purity tends in the end to a cult of gloom, a hatred of life, and worse still to a systematic effort to degrade and destroy one of the most precious of God's gifts to man. The result of this degradation can never be the flowering of a "more spiritual" and more self-sacrificing love but only a shameful and destructive counterfeit.

It is, of course, true that many honest and well-meaning men and women have, through God's mercy, become saints due to the suffering that was imposed on them by their inhuman concept of love—held in perfectly good faith. But let us not say they were sanctified *by* this concept. They were sanctified *in spite* of it.

Platonism is blamed, not without reason, for some of the exaggerations of the view we have described. But let us not forget that Platonism has to be seen in its own social and cultural context, which is not that of our day.

The ancient Platonic view of purity, which possessed a certain distinction of its own, was aristocratic and contemplative. It associated the purity of the "theoretical" mind with leisure that was not defiled by workaday concerns and with speculation that was able to rise above the limitations of matter. In this context, the "pure" mind was that which was not bound to images and material concepts, but rose freely to the realm of pure ideas and essences, unimpeded by any obstacle. The pure mind was detached, tranquil, not easily distracted. In some contexts, this purity was mathematical and scientific. In others, aesthetic. Or in others, ethical. The early Christian monastic tradition with its emphasis on "purity of heart" applied this Platonic scheme to the Christian contemplative life and to the search for "mystical theology" or union with God beyond all concepts and created essences in the dark night of pure contemplation.

Since in this tradition it was generally understood that involvement both in manual labor and in the sexuality of married life tended to be an obstacle to contemplation, it was assumed that work, married love, and active concerns of civic life were less "pure" than the leisure and abstraction of the theoretic life. In order to seek this "purity," ascetics even left the world altogether and fled into the nakedness of the desert, where there were the least possible obstacles to the direct ascent of the mind to God. This was the pure life par excellence, the *bios angelikos,* or the life of the angels (which are of course "pure spirits").

It may be mentioned here that the concept of Platonic love —a purely spiritual eroticism—was also highly sophisticated and complex and must be seen in the climate of an aristocratic culture in which *eros* was by no means left systematically disincarnate! Unfortunately, this idealism tended to make a drastic separation between the love of the ideal woman (spiritual) and the love of a prostitute or mistress (fleshly and passionate).

We have now examined two concepts of purity, one of which is morally decadent, the other of which, though noble and respectable, is antiquated and presupposes an entirely different world view from that in which we live. Can the concept of purity be salvaged at all for our time?

To begin with, is it worth salvaging? This depends on what you are trying to save and restore. Obviously, there is no point in brushing up a dusty and rather dreadful old bit of ethical furniture and putting it back in the living room with the Mondrians and the mobile. But, on the other hand, there is a certain ideal of human integrity in love and in life which was once served by this notion, and can perhaps be served again. Here we must, of course, get rid of all confusion between "purity" and mere respectability or even decency. The existentialists have, in fact, opened up a fairly useful approach to this problem, and if we see that in their idea of the *authentic* use of human freedom they have salvaged some of the value under consideration, we can appreciate what "purity" might conceivably mean for us. Mechanically speaking, we will arrive at this, not by *dividing* as the Platonists did, but by amalgamating, integrating, bringing together. The area in which this most needs to be done is, of course, that of sexual love.

For example, instead of saying that an act is pure when you *remove* all that is material, sensuous, fleshly, emotional, passionate, etc., from it, we will on the contrary say that a sexual act is pure when it gives a rightful place to the body, the senses, the emotions (conscious and unconscious), the special needs of the person, all that is called for by the unique relationship between the two lovers, and what is demanded by the situation in which they find themselves. The aim is not to establish in the stuffiest possible way the full legality of their act of love but to liberate in them all the capacity for love and for the expression of love that would be truly and fully authentic in their peculiar circumstances. And this, of course, would be decided not so much by abstract legal norms (which nevertheless have their objective function and their role in guiding the individual) but also by personal conscience and decision in the light of grace and of the providential demands of one's love.

Here it must be very clearly stated that an uninhibited erotic love between married persons not only can be pure but will most probably be *more pure* than an anguished, constrained, and painful attack by an embarrassed husband on his patient and inert wife. The act of sexual love should by its very nature be joyous, unconstrained, alive, leisurely, inventive, and full of a special delight which the lovers have learned by experience to create for one another. There is no more beautiful gift of God than the little secret world of creative love and expression in which two persons who have totally surrendered to each other manifest and celebrate their mutual gift. *It is precisely in this spirit of celebration, gratitude, and joy that true purity is found.* The pure heart is not one that is terrified of eros but one that, with the confidence and abandon of a child of God, accepts this gift as a sacred trust, for sex, too, is one of the talents which Christ has left us to trade with until He returns. Properly understood sexual union is an expression of deep personal love and a means to the deepening, perfecting, and sanctifying of that love. To seek sexual gratification as an end in itself and without due regard for the needs of one's partner would make this true purity of love almost impossible. Therefore, it is immediately apparent that the notion of purity in love can be fully guaranteed only by a maturely developed sense of personal sacrifice for the good of the other and in order to meet the deepest and most challenging demands of the situation. Here the purity of love will be discovered not by the mechanical application of merely external norms but by a wise and even inspired integration of personal freedom and objective demands, so that the act of love will flower into a more fruitful and creative expression of life and truth. Such purity must, of course, be judged objectively, not merely by the subjective needs and desires of the lovers, and the standard of objective judgment will be, for instance, the *wholeness* of the act of love. That act will be pure which in all its aspects can be said to respect the truth and integrity, the true needs and the deepest good of those who share it together, as well as the objective demands of others, of society and so on.

By this standard, certain casuistical interpretations which would permit an unhealthy and truncated sexual activity as still legally "pure" will be seen as an affront to the authentic wholeness and purity of man. Others which might from a certain point of view shock and scandalize conventional minds may nevertheless meet a profoundly authentic and spiritual demand for inner purity and wholeness. But we cannot say that the individual person is left entirely to his own judgment in each case. The last court of appeal is not subjective freedom, which can easily become arbitrary and lead to just as many appalling truncations as legalism does. The mark of love is its respect for reality and for truth and its concern for the values which it must foster, preserve, and increase in the world. Such concern is not compatible with fantasy, willfulness, or the neglect of the rights and needs of other people.

In this new approach to purity, the emphasis will be not so much on law as on love, not so much on what happens to nature or to the parts of the body as to what develops in the person (though in this case the two are manifestly inseparable). We must consider not so much what is acceptable in a social milieu as what will truly provide a creative and intimately personal solution to the questions raised in each special case.

This concept of purity is, therefore, not one in which two people seek to love each other in spirit and truth *in spite* of their bodies, but, on the contrary, use all the resources of body, mind, heart, imagination, emotion, and will in order to celebrate the love that has been given them by God, and in so doing to praise Him!

V World

Christians are now asking themselves curious questions about something called the "world." Should they revile it as their fathers did? Should they renounce it as monks do? Should they love it as it loves itself? Should they enter into dialogue with it, as the Pope has dialogues with all kinds of people not excluding Russians? Or, in the long run, should they frankly admit that they are part of the world and start from there? What is this world? Does it exist at all?

We must begin by frankly admitting that the first place in which to go looking for the world is not outside us but in ourselves. We *are* the world. In the deepest ground of our being we remain in metaphysical contact with the whole of that creation in which we are only small parts. Through our senses and our minds, our loves, needs, and desires, we are implicated, without possibility of evasion, in this world of matter and of men, of things and of persons, which not only affect us and change our lives but are also affected and changed by us. From the moment we sit down at the table and put a piece of bread in our mouths, we see that we are in the world and cannot be otherwise than in it, until the day we die. The question, then, is not to speculate about how we are to contact the world—as if we were somehow in outer space—but how to validate our relationship, give it a fully honest and human significance, and make it truly productive and worthwhile for our world.

Yet at the same time we must also recognize that we are all able to distinguish between ourselves and the world, since we are all capable of recognizing the mystery of our own subjective identity. Furthermore, we intuitively grasp the fact that this identity affirms and builds itself by a kind of dialectic of love, understanding, work, and communion with the "rest of the world." It is, in fact, essential to human consciousness to begin with the distinction between "I" and "all the rest of the world," and as everyone keeps pointing out since Martin Buber, this must grow and resolve itself into an "I-Thou" relationship with the other. Without this perfection of dialogue and love, the "I" will be forever deprived, alienated, and isolated in a world that is either hostile and incomprehensible or totally devouring.

It would be interesting to trace the whole history of this concept of a temporal material world to which man felt free to oppose himself, which he could stand against, from which he could separate himself, declare himself free, against which he could choose to act, or which he was able to parley with. It doubtless goes back to the great discovery of personal identity and freedom in the age of the Greek city-states, of the Hebrew Prophets, of Buddha and Zoroaster, of Confucius and Lao-tse. Not that all these had the same concept of "the world," but they all in one way or another saw man as able to distinguish himself from what was merely "there" and "given" in order to make up his own mind and adopt his own attitudes toward it.

Hence, to really understand the old traditional ideas of "contempt for the world," we must see them in the light of their correlatives. The man who was able to contemn the world, that is, to affirm his own independence of servitude to the "given," was proclaiming his respect for the free person. This in its turn redounded to the world's advantage in the long run because the free person, instead of submitting blindly to stereotyped patterns and familiar ways, felt himself called to develop new ways and new attitudes, and eventually to make new discoveries which changed the world. Contempt for the world was in reality the first beginning of love for the world, and the great religions which taught flight from the world also laid the foundation for world views which established man in the world as its master and its renewer.

What, then, is the world? Simply the human and non-human environment in which man finds himself, to which he is called to establish a certain definite relationship. It is true that most men are content to accept a ready-made relationship which the world itself offers them, but in theory we are all free to stand back from the world, to judge it, and even to come to certain decisions about remaking it. At least we can do this in the little world with which we surround ourselves in our own nests—our homes.

Man's ordinary dialogue with the world in this sense is called *work*. This is without doubt the fundamental dialogue in which all should participate, and when they cannot, then something goes radically wrong with the non-participants and with the world itself. One of the great problems of our century is not merely that of finding work for the unemployed but that of developing a new concept of work that will prevent practically everybody from becoming unemployable.

It is clear that work also conventionally regards the world as an opponent to be dealt with by ingenuity and strength, indeed to be "overcome," though this highly aggressive image is more proper to Western society, in which it has developed beyond reason.

But man's environment is not simply made up of natural and physical forces, of societies moved by orderly economic laws, and so forth. There is a world within the world, and this other world is quite a different affair. It is much more mysterious and much less easy to "stand over against," to resist and to challenge. On the contrary, this other world offers an easy solution to the man who wants to fabricate a crude identity for himself without too much trouble and with a minimum of personal responsibility. This world says, "Work with me and I will take care of your identity." It is a world with which, in other words, we are summoned to make a more radical and disquieting identification. It demands our total submission—the abdication of our freedom. This world is a complex dynamic of power, of need, of ambition, of obsession with gain and with lust. It is particularly marked by obliviousness to and contempt for all that does not fit in with its own peculiar power constellation. It has no patience with anyone who does not totally submit to and identify with that constellation. Typologically, this world in the Bible is

Egypt and Babylon, the realm of the greater and more inhuman servitudes. It is the kingdom of Satan, which is by
that very fact opposed to the liberty of the City of God. When
the New Testament speaks of the world as a realm to be
rejected, resisted, fled from, defied, it speaks of the world as
this constellation of power, lust, and greed. The most difficult
of ambiguities for the Christian today arises where, in his
genuine and well-meant desire to enter into dialogue with the
world, he simply goes through the old gestures of submission
to Pharaoh without which the world does not even begin to
speak to anyone at all.

Finally, there is the true world of the Christian, the world
as redeemed by Christ and transfigured from within by a history which the power constellation does not recognize but
which nevertheless is the true history of the world. In this
redeemed world, which is the only true world, the Christian
can understand his relationship to the world of power. He
does not have to enter into a contest with the world of power
for anything but his own independence. Once he is free, he
sees that the entire redeemed world is his, in Christ, and he
need not dispute it with anyone.

The Christian's dialogue with the world can, then, be
summed up as follows: First, he is created in the world. The
world of his time is the place of salvation to which he has
been called by God, in which God has put him, in which God
has a task for him to accomplish. If he merely rejects and
disparages the world of matter in which he is, the Christian
can never really begin to understand his task in it, and he will
not be able to do the work God asks of him.

Second, however, he must stand back from the world as
power constellation demanding absolute submission and servitude. Here the Christian must face the awful fact that, in
certain historical compromises with power, churchmen have
seemed to identify the Church itself with the worldly power

constellation, and as a result of this, there are terrible ambiguities laid upon the Christian conscience. For example, in the question of war, which is the paradigm of all "worldly activity" in the sense of action within the power constellation. The symbolic refusal of the martyrs to worship idols in the Roman Empire may call for an equally symbolic and significant refusal on the part of Christians today in making clear their independence of structures ordered to brute power. But these ambiguities are the most painful and complex problems of the Christian conscience in our time.

Third, it is when the Christian learns to recognize the world as redeemed and enters into an "I-Thou" relationship with all other persons in it seen as loved and sought by Christ that he obtains spiritual leverage to free the world from the tyranny of its own worldliness.

There is no simple "ethical" answer to the problems arising from this attitude. The Christian does not learn a new set of unworldly laws which he opposes to the ways of the world, but by the Cross and Love of Christ and the indwelling Spirit of freedom, he learns to live in the world as Christ did, in perfect liberty and with unlimited compassion and service.

VI Ethics

Is the practical science of ethics to be taken seriously? The question is no doubt confusing, for while we still assume that men do, in fact, seek to base their conduct on certain moral dictates which have an objective basis and which are recognizable to a mature conscience, we are also sometimes uneasily aware of a certain pseudoseriousness in ethical exhortation. This pseudoseriousness seems to be due in part to the insecurity of minds troubled by the enormous confusion of modern thought. One always wants to do "what is right," and one is always confronted with completely contradictory ethical imperatives. Though A is incompatible with B, both A and B can advance arguments to show why they alone should be chosen. The only real "seriousness" that a mature ethical knowledge can trust today is the unseriousness of a profound humility and openness which is ready to commit itself to the risk of provisional decisions where moral norms no longer seem absolutely certain in themselves. In other words, an ethical seriousness which bases itself on the absolute validity of its own system tends in the end to be pseudoserious and confusing. An ethic of personal integrity and responsibility is more practical. But such an ethic cannot be purely subjective. It accepts and respects objective moral norms, while remembering the distinction between an objective norm and a pathological compulsion. A mature conscience is one which is willing to risk the responsibility of committing itself to action based on norms which are reasonable and sane but which do not always lay claim to an infallible and invariable validity. In this case, it is the person who assumes responsibility for his own act. He does not transfer all responsibility to the laws and moral dictates which he has chosen to obey.

But what are these moral dictates? Are they simply pragmatic conventions? Are they merely deduced from the requirements of this or that social system? Are they no more than gestures of conformity which are assumed to be at once useful and commendable, like traffic laws? We live, in fact, in a world in which ethical principles tend to become extremely hazy and even to be entirely forgotten or discredited. In concrete situations in which moral law claims a hearing, we often hear protests against the "impracticality" of its demands, and where these demands are respected, it is often quite grudgingly, as if they were no more than the sentimental velleities for inner comfort entertained by people who have no stomach for the hard facts of life.

For example, moral protest on the part of civilians who

object to inhuman methods of warfare are greeted with indignant incomprehension by the military, who conceive that the purpose of war is simply to annihilate the enemy and everything he stands for. Machiavelli long ago pointed out how, in fact, ethics fatally obstruct the efficiency of military tactics. His advice to princes was to forget ethics entirely and to make no pretense of being "moral." Even this, however, is a kind of "ethic" in its own way.

Ethics is a practical science of attaining one's ends as a human being. One's ethics will, then, depend on his anthropology and on his metaphysic. Where neither anthropology nor metaphysic has ever been heard of, then ethics will be nothing more than a set of slogans designed to justify pure expediency.

The ends which ethics as a practical science must clarify are the specific ends of man as man, in the fullness of his humanity, and in all his personal freedom and responsibility. The science of ethics then teaches us not merely how to get whatever we want without falling foul of civil and criminal law but to live in such a way that our actions will make us more perfectly human and enable us to discover ourselves in the fullest measure as free persons. With this purpose, ethics studies norms of conduct which will enable us realistically to accomplish our vital human task. Moral norms must first of all be concrete and objective. They are discovered within man himself, and above all in his relationships with other men. They are found to be constant and universal, though in many cases admitting exceptions and qualifications. Training in ethics means, then, not only the study of these norms, but also the formation of a personal and mature conscience which can make practical judgments in applying moral norms to the problematic situations of life. Although the moral law in the abstract may be perfectly clear, its concrete application in difficult cases will always be full of risk, because we can never be quite sure that we fully understand the object of our choice, its real end, and all the circumstances surrounding it. Therefore, ethical conduct (prudent conduct) calls for the advice of others who have knowledge and experience of the problems we confront. Yet there will always be cases where the person must ultimately decide in the solitude of his own conscience, never perfectly sure that he fully understands what he is doing. In such a case, ethical conduct implies something beyond ethics—prayer, faith, and trust in God. Ethics is, then, not simply a code of rules by which one learns to play social games; it aims at the complete formation of the human person. In addition to knowing the objective norms of conduct, one must also acquire a kind of intuitive sense of how to put them into practice in individual circumstances. Here ethics blends into the art of living, and becomes, in fact, the education of human love.

We must, of course, point out that mere ethics, as a moral philosophy, has its limitations. It needs to be completed by a higher science that apprehends other and more mysterious norms which have been revealed to man by God and which arise out of the deep personal relation of man to God in saving grace, by which man is oriented to his true and perfect finality: his ultimate fulfillment as a person in the love of God and of his fellow man in God. This is the science of moral and mystical theology.

If ethics tend to be discredited, it may be partly because moral philosophers have been too absolute and not realistic enough in their view of man. An obsessive cult of abstract norms and of disembodied duty may reduce ethical science and conduct to an exercise of will, divorced from every other human consideration and value. Man is then alienated from himself and forced to live, as Bonhoeffer said, "in the glaring and fatiguing light of incessant consciousness." In reality, this points to a failure of the true ethical sense, that intuitive appreciation of the human values which ethics are meant to preserve.

The more abstract and idealistic an ethical system is, the more it will tend, in fact, to devaluate and to reject life, substituting for it a cult of moral myths and abstractions that have no relation to the true purpose of man's development. Such ethical systems can easily become so perverse that instead of helping man to truly find and develop his freedom in authentic love, they convince him that his highest values are to be sought in the refusal of himself and of love. This begets a morality of self-hate, of resentment, of frustration, of meanness and gloom. It is nothing more than an apotheosis of the death wish and a pure hatred of life.

This compulsive rejection of the concrete self with its natural needs and demands is generally made in the name of an ideal self which is conceived as impossibly righteous and pure, and which can never be realized in fact. Yet one persists in trying to live an impossible and self-destructive life in pursuit of this ideal. When ethical systems thus betray their own purpose, they are themselves responsible for the fact that morality is discredited and becomes totally meaningless to new generations which must grope for fulfillment outside the barren area illuminated by its glaring and inhuman light.

VII War

Living in a world that is constantly at war, in an age when all war has become total war, we scarcely need an explanation of what war is. And yet we are so familiar with it that we forget what it really is. If we did not forget so easily, we would not be so ready to become involved in new ones.

The most obvious fact about war today is that while everyone claims to hate it, and all are unanimously agreed that it is our greatest single evil, there is little significant resistance to it except on the part of small minorities who, by the very fact of their protest, are dismissed as eccentric. The awful fact is that though mankind fears war and seeks to avoid it, the fear is irrational and inefficacious. It can do nothing against a profound *unconscious proclivity to violence* which seems, in fact, to be one of the most mysterious characteristics of man, not only in his individuality, but in his collective and social life. War represents a vice that mankind would like to get rid of but which it cannot do without. Man is like an alcoholic who knows that drink will destroy him but who always has a reason for drinking. So with war. And the best, most obvious, most incontrovertible reason for war is of course "peace." The motive for which men are led to fight today is that war is necessary to destroy those who threaten our peace! It should be clear from this that war is, in fact, totally irrational, and that it proceeds to its violent ritual with the chanting of perfect nonsense. Yet men not only accept this, they even go so far as to sacrifice their lives and their human dignity and to commit the most hideous atrocities, convinced that in so doing they are being noble, honest, self-sacrificing, and just.

The only possible conclusion is that man is so addicted to war that he cannot possibly deal with his addiction. And yet if he does not learn to cope with it, the addiction will ruin him altogether.

Instead of dealing in abstractions, let us begin by considering the typical and concrete act of war: the destruction of Dresden, by the English and Americans, in the Second World War.

First of all, it must be remembered that considerably more people were killed in this bombing raid than in the atom bombing of Hiroshima or Nagasaki. In wave after wave of bombers, the defenseless city of Dresden was systematically pulverized and reduced to ashes by so-called conventional weapons—which no longer excite any special interest on the part of casuists today.

Second, Dresden was not what one could call a military target, and in any case, the bombers paid no special attention to the industrial plants in and around the city. They concentrated on the city itself and the residential areas. In so doing, they obtained what someone referred to as a "bonus" in extra victims, since the city was filled with refugees flying from the Russian Army in the east.

Third, the bombing of Dresden was not necessary, nor was it even from a military point of view particularly useful. Dresden was bombed for purely political reasons, glossed over perhaps with arguments for military expediency.

In a word, this ferocious and massive act of destruction was nothing but a calculated atrocity, perpetrated for the effect that it might have on the Russian ally. But as ever in such cases, it was rationalized as an inescapable necessity.

It will be seen that anyone who willingly participates in modern warfare sooner or later commits himself to cooperation in acts like this.

For this reason, Pope John XXIII, in *Pacem in Terris,* declared that war was no longer to be considered a rational method of settling international disputes (since it obviously settles nothing at all), and the Second Vatican Council called for an entirely new evaluation of war on the part of all the men of our time, in the realization that we will all be called upon to account for our acts of war and the future will depend on the decisions we make today (*Constitution on the Church in the Modern World,* n. 80). The Council added:

> Any act of war aimed indiscriminately at the destruction of entire cities or extensive areas along with their population is a crime against God and man himself. It merits unequivocal and unhesitating condemnation (*ibid.*).

The arms race is an utterly treacherous trap for humanity and one which ensnares the poor to an intolerable degree. It is much to be feared that, if this race persists, it will eventually spawn all the lethal ruin whose path it is now making possible . . . Divine Providence urgently demands of us that we free ourselves from the age-old slavery of war . . . It is our clear duty therefore to strain every muscle in working for the time when all war can be completely outlawed by international consent (*ibid.* 82).

What the Council has said is, of course, quite obvious to reason. But we repeat, the trouble is that war is not made by reason, its conduct is not governed by reason. To appeal against war to reason is to make an appeal that cannot have any serious effect on the war makers themselves.

Though sustaining itself by a massive pseudologic of its own, war is, in fact, a complete suspension of reason. This is at once its danger and the source of its immense attraction. War is by its nature supposed to be the "last resort" when, all reasoning having failed, men must turn to force to decide their differences. The moral problem of war does not begin when men have finally resorted to force. The root problem of war is *the occult determination to resort to force in any case,* and the more or less conscious self-frustration of any show of "reason" in settling the problem that will eventually be decided by the ordeal of force. The awful danger of war is, then, not so much that force is used when reason has broken down but that reason unconsciously inhibits itself beforehand (in all the trivialities of political and military gamesmanship) *in order that it may break down, and in order that resort to force may become "inevitable."*

This demonic psychological mechanism behind war is at once the fault of everybody and of nobody. The individuals who make the actual decisions are convinced that they are acting seriously and responsibly, and indeed they can convincingly display the anguish they feel in their awful situation. The public applauds their sacrifice and clamors for guns and ammunition. And yet: when examined dispassionately by the historian, it may often be seen how "inevitable" wars could fairly easily have been avoided. If only whole nations had not been ready to fight, if only empires had not thirsted for blood and revenge, if only the commanders had not been all too eager for a pretext to launch another campaign!

The real problem of war is, then, not to be found in this or that special way in which force is grossly abused, but in the instinct for violence and for resort to force which has become inveterate in the human race. Is this something that man can learn to change? If so, how does he go about it? What should he do? Where should the study of this dreadful problem begin? Who can say?

Perhaps our first problem is to get rid of the illusion that we know the answer.

III
CHRISTIAN HUMANISM

Christian Humanism

The topic of Christian humanism must be frankly faced by the Christian today as both problem and temptation. A problem because the very possibility of an authentic Christian humanism is questioned by a secular culture, a culture of revolution, which declares religion to be a social mystification which diminishes man's human stature, blunts his creativity, and retards his growth toward maturity. This, of course, suggests the temptation: the easy answer which can be drawn from the Christian humanism and culture of the past.

Anyone who has seriously studied the Christian culture of the thousand years between the Patristic Age and the Renaissance knows well enough how it abounded in life, sanity, joy, and creative power. Only those who are still clinging to nineteenth-century clichés can still regard the Middle Ages as a time of unrelieved darkness.

There is no doubt whatever, even in the minds of those who attack Christianity, that the culture of medieval Christendom and the humanism of the Christian and European Renaissance represent decisive steps in man's growth. This culture was responsible for the formation of our present world—with all its glories and all its blemishes. But this facile recourse to the past might well be both ambiguous and insincere.

Why ambiguous? Not because of the paradox of a "Christian humanism" which at the same time denied the world and affirmed it. This is a curious and quite sophisticated cultural phenomenon which is incidentally in one way or another common to all the great spiritual world religions. Even in Buddhism, which is far more radically world-denying than Christianity, one finds an exquisite affirmation of life and of human values. The student of these religions knows well that having established a certain *distance* and *freedom,* by means of detachment, their believers were able to love the world all the more freely and purely because they were liberated from it. So, too, with the Christian Saints. But this is not the ambiguity I mean.

Because of the historical complexity and the many-sidedness of Christian culture, it has become all too easy for the Christian apologist to have things both ways, and indeed to advance a ready explanation for almost anything. Science? Technology? Humanism? Progress? Evolution? Even revolution? One can always point to some Christian who has distinguished himself by devotion to one or another of these and infer, without further argument, that *all* Christians are just on the point of agreeing with him unanimously.

After all, it is not enough to have a saint for everything. It is not enough to display Thomas More as the example of the Christian humanism, the layman, the statesman, the father of the family, the student of the classics, and the friend of Erasmus (who himself is unfortunately not on display as another humanist saint, since for various obscure reasons he could not quite make it). Nor is it enough to repeat once again the familiar arguments about the culture of medieval monks. What point is there in asserting today that though St. Gregory the Great did not like the *Grammar* of Donatus, he was nevertheless a gifted and well-informed writer in his own way? Or that the fulminations of St. Jerome and St. Peter Damian against the liberal arts did not prevent them from being well formed in the classic curriculum. There are better and more uncompromising examples of Christian openness to all forms of profane knowledge in the Middle Ages—the School of Chartres, for instance, with its platonizing scholars, who were also deeply intrigued by the natural world. The School of St. Victor, which declared, "Learn everything, you will find nothing superfluous." Above all, there is St. Thomas and his openness to Aristotle, to the Arabs, and to the claims of reason, nature, and man.

Yet a historical apologetic is not conclusive. It is unfortunate that the Renaissance Popes and their love of art do not offer completely convincing arguments for Christian humanism when we remember the unfortunate Galileo affair. To go further and declare that Christian humanism is a living force in the world today simply because this world remains in cultural continuity with the Christendom of the past would, in fact, be quite equivocal. Let us not forget that certain writers have coined the invidious phrase "post-Christian world" to designate our age, in which the moral climate is poisoned by a residue of once Christian values that have now been perverted and abandoned. We will not pause here to debate about this provocative concept.

Our problem is not so much to celebrate the supposedly acquired and well-established glories of an eternal humanism stamped with the seal of classic reason and ennobled by Christian faith. We face the much more disquieting task of inquiring under what conditions Christians can establish, by their outlook and their action in the world of today, the claim to be true participants in the building of a new humanism. Hence, it is a matter not so much of giving an obvious answer to an often-repeated question as of asking ourselves whether we Christians are really in a position to understand questions that are in their way altogether new, and whether our Christian faith can suggest appropriate and original answers.

The thesis of this article is that Christianity can not only throw light on the most typical and most urgent problems of the modern world but that there is a certain light which Christianity alone can provide. But this light does not shine all by itself. It is not always clearly apparent to the world in official statements and declarations of the Church, but it must be made evident by the creative activity of Christians themselves as they participate in the solution of contemporary problems on which the very future of man depends. There must be no mistake about it: at a time when the progress and perhaps even the very survival of mankind depend on the solution of certain grave problems which are basically ethical as well as economic and political, Christianity can and must contribute something of its own unique and irreplaceable insights into the value of man, not only in his human nature, but in his inalienable dignity as a free person. The course of these insights is, of course, redemptive love.

Unfortunately, the true Christian concept of love has sometimes been discredited by those who have sentimentalized it, or formalized it in one way or another. A sincere subjective disposition to love everyone does not dispense from energetic and sacrificial social action to restore violated rights to the oppressed, to create work for the workless, so that the hungry may eat and that everyone may have a chance to earn a decent wage. It has unfortunately been all too easy in the past for the man who is himself well fed to entertain the most laudable sentiments of love for his neighbor, while ignoring the fact that his brother is struggling to solve insoluble and tragic problems.

Mere almsgiving is no longer adequate, especially if it is only a gesture which seems to dispense from all further and more efficacious social action. This is not always, of course, a question of genuine insincerity: but the "good works" that measured up to the needs of small medieval communities can no longer serve in the fantastic and worldwide crisis that is sweeping all mankind today, when the population of the world is counted in billions, which double in forty, twenty, and then fifteen years. In such a case, the dimensions of Christian love must be expanded and universalized on the same scale as the human problem that is to be met. The individual gesture, however commendable, will no longer suffice.

The Second Vatican Council clearly recognized the revolutionary character of the modern world in which we are entering into a "new age of human history. New ways are open therefore for the perfection and further extension of culture. These ways have been prepared by the enormous growth of natural, human and social sciences, and by technical progress" (*Constitution on the Church in the Modern World,* n. 54). "More and more men," the Council continued, become conscious of their great role as "authors and artisans of the culture of their community," and it concludes: "Thus we are witnesses of the birth of a new humanism, one in which man is defined first of all by his responsibility to his brothers and to history" (n. 55). It is evident that Christian humanism itself now takes on a new aspect, and any Christian who appeals to the medieval forms of Christian humanism, as if they were opposed to the new, cannot help but make the message of the Council sound confused and ambiguous. Nothing must obscure the obligation of the Christian *"to work with all men in the building of a more human world"* (n. 57). Such is the explicit teaching of the Catholic Church today.

It is, therefore, extremely important to get rid of a profound confusion that identifies the Christian culture and world view of Western society from the fall of Rome to the French Revolution with "Christianity" pure and simple. This world view, which, as we have seen, was in its own way profoundly humanistic, was nevertheless hemmed in by certain limitations. It tended to regard man and the universe as static and definitively given realities which do not change in any important sense: realities which simply have to be understood and accepted in their unchanging natures. The dynamism of historic development was underestimated, and all profound social change was regarded with suspicion and indeed with implacable hostility.

A certain theology of Providence was developed in this milieu, and today we must perhaps re-examine this theology, distinguishing in it those elements which simply reflected the culture and society of the time from those which are truly revealed by God. For instance, must one assume that all man's historic development simply conforms to a rigidly predetermined plan that has already been worked out in all its details? Must we consider that the only function of man's freedom is to discover and accept what has already been imposed upon him by God without any consideration for his own creative possibilities? Does this predetermined plan simply crush all initiative, so that, in fact, new and creative ideas are to be regarded as rebellious and erroneous by the very fact that they are new?

Anyone who has read the Prophets and the New Testament with any attention recognizes that one of the most essential facts about Christianity is that, being a religion of love, it is also at the same time a religion of dynamic change.

If we consider the true meaning of the first word in the Christian message of salvation, *metanoiete,* "repent," we see that it is a summons to a complete change of life both for the individual and for society. This change did not take place, once for all, two thousand years ago. The summons to change, to man's creative self-realization and development in the spirit, as a child of God whom the truth shall make free, *is a summons to permanent newness of life.* The true concept of

Christian order is, then, something much more dynamic and modern than the classical hierarchic pyramid with God at the top, man halfway down, and prime matter at the bottom—an order in which each one has a fixed place determined for him eternally before he was born. In such a context, the call to repent is simply a call to assume one's proper place in the cosmic order—in a word, a rather minor adjustment which in many cases amounts to nothing more than accepting what one already has and not protesting or asking for more. One of the historic paradoxes that resulted from this fixation of the Christian world view in one static concept is that the dynamic aspect of Christianity was left to be rediscovered and emphasized by thinkers who stood outside Christian institutions and were highly critical of them.

In reality, the criticism leveled against Christianity by Feuerbach and Marx can be seen as having occultly Christian elements which need to be taken seriously. Religion is for Marx essentially a process of mystification and alienation, in which man accepts estrangement from himself, projects his own reality outside himself, impoverishes himself, and dehumanizes himself, in order to lead what is essentially a fantasy life centered on the abstract idea of God. God is in a remote heaven where he will one day reward man. This fantasy life of religion, with its complex of beliefs and observances, is then substituted for the real, productive, creative life in which man ought to take his own world in hand and, instead of merely thinking about it and dreaming about it, actually set about changing it, and thereby changing himself. It is not in constructing a religious system of ideology and worship that intervenes between himself and his real world that man can find truth and happiness. No, says Marx, he must enter into a direct and concrete relationship with his world of matter, with his brother, and with himself. Man humanizes both himself and his world by working to better the conditions of all men in the world. Hence, according to Marx, religious ideologies and formalities of worship prevent man from being himself, prevent him from being human, and consequently there can be no such thing as a religious humanism. The first step to any authentic humanism is the rejection of religion.

This is a very telling historic criticism, and unless the Christian is willing to face it, there is no further point in talking about Christian humanism today. But actually it is not a difficult criticism to face. To begin with, it rests on a deep but perfectly understandable misconception about the true essence of Christianity. Marx was not only following Feuerbach's critique of Hegel's essentially un-Christian theology but also accepting as "Christian" the superficial and decadent manifestations of Christianity which he saw around him in early-nineteenth-century Germany and which he did not bother to examine in any depth. There is no question that if pseudo-Christianity is taken to be "Christian," one can with the greatest of ease destroy all its claims to being humanistic.

On the other hand, one has only to open the New Testament at random and one will almost immediately discover the clearest evidence that the preaching of Jesus and the teaching of the Apostles were directed precisely against what we have come to know as religious alienation. Useless to multiply quotations here: a typical one, "The sabbath was made for man, not man for the sabbath" (Mark 2:27), evokes the whole struggle of Jesus with the Pharisees about the question of sabbath observance. In each case, what is of utmost importance is the fact that Jesus, for instance, in working miracles on the sabbath, is emphasizing the priority of human values over conventionally "religious" ones. In each case, where there is a choice between the good of a suffering human person and the claims of formal and established legalism, Jesus decides for the person and against the claims of legalistic religion.

It is extremely important to see that the issue can be stated in such blunt and stark terms. "Religion clean and undefiled before God and the Father is this, to visit the fatherless and widows in their tribulation . . ." (James 1:27). All through the New Testament we find the explicit contrast between a mere interior religiosity, abstract, mental, and intentional, or even purely a matter of fantasy, and that love which, in uniting man to his brother of flesh and blood, thereby also unites him to the truth in God (John 13:34–35; 1 John 4:7–11).

How does man attain to a real union of love with his neighbor? Not merely by abstract agreement about truths concerning the end of all things and the afterlife, but by a realistic collaboration in the work of daily living in the world of hard facts in which man must work in order to eat. This is clearly shown in St. Paul's Epistles to the Thessalonians, among whom a certain type of apocalyptic thinking tended to substitute the speculations of pseudomysticism for the everyday task of the Christian in his world (1 Thessalonians 4:11; 2 Thessalonians 3:6–15). We find here that Paul protests against a religious alienation which substitutes a mental life of religious ideas for a practical Christian life of love in the midst of everyday realities.

The fact that the New Testament provides a theological basis for the practical life of love among men does nothing to weaken that love and certainly does not make it abstract. The Christian loves because *God is love,* and because God is manifested in actual love, not only in pious ideas and practices. Indeed, God does not wish to remain isolated in a remote heaven. He has willed to come down and "pitch his tent" among men *in order to manifest himself in man.* Furthermore, he wills to do this *only with the free cooperation of man himself.* One of the most fundamental ideas of Christianity is that the free decision of men to love one another in Christ enables them to cooperate positively and creatively in the definitive manifestation of God on earth (John 17:3–23).

This is precisely the "new commandment" which is at the heart of the "new covenant" or "New Testament," that is to say, the new relationship between man and God, the very essence of the teaching of Christianity. The teaching of the Gospel is that men are no longer servants of God, no longer bound merely to complex ritual observances and obscure legal systems known only to experts. Men are free from the domination of abstract religious systems that can only be understood by specialists. They are sons of God and brothers of one another, united in a community of freedom and love in which their law is love and in which they are guided by the Spirit of God dwelling in the Church and in each of its members— the Spirit of sonship, of freedom, and of love.

The Epistles of St. Paul, particularly those to the Romans and the Galatians, can and should be read as tracts against what we call religious alienation. These writings are clear affirmations of man in his full freedom as a son of God. The whole meaning of the Cross, for Paul, is that in Christ man has died to the law and risen to a new life of liberty from sin (i.e., selfishness). In Christ, man received a new identity as a son of God in the Spirit of divine love. He is now no longer the wretched alienated slave who lives enclosed in a world of superstitions and fear-ridden ideas. He is a free man. He has now become Christ the Son of God (Galatians 2:19–20). The message of faith preached by Paul is not simply a set of obscure answers to questions about the other world and the afterlife: what is demanded of the Christian, above all, is that he believe that it is possible for him to be a son of God in Christ. He must clearly understand that he does not have to keep an ancient ritual law in order to please God (Galatians 3:1–3). The heart of true Christian humanism, in its full theological dimension, is to be sought in the revealed doctrine of the Incarnation, man's sonship of God in Christ, and the gift of the Holy Spirit as a principle of divine life and love in man. The Church is the center and focus of this incarnational and redemptive humanism because it is in her that Christ dwells, and the transforming power of the Holy Spirit makes men into sons of God.

Above all, we must understand the crucial importance of *forgiveness* as the heart of Christian humanism. Christianity is not merely a religious system which attempts to *explain* evil; it is a life of dynamic love which *forgives* evil and, by forgiving, enables love to transform evil into good. *The dynamic of Christian love is a dynamic of forgiveness,* and the true secret of Christian humanism is that it has the divine power to transform man in the very ground of his being from a miserable enslaved and confused being into a free son of God. This divine transforming power is forgiveness, Christian mercy. Where this merciful love is absent, there can no longer be any claim to an authentic Christianity (1 Corinthians 13:1–3).

"IF I SPEAK IN THE TONGUES OF MEN AND OF ANGELS, BUT HAVE NOT LOVE, I AM A NOISY GONG OR A CLANGING CYMBAL. AND IF I HAVE PROPHETIC POWERS, AND UNDERSTAND ALL MYSTERIES AND ALL KNOWLEDGE, AND IF I HAVE ALL FAITH, SO AS TO REMOVE MOUNTAINS, BUT HAVE NOT LOVE, I AM NOTHING. IF I GIVE AWAY ALL I HAVE, AND IF I DELIVER MY BODY TO BE BURNED, BUT HAVE NOT LOVE, I GAIN NOTHING."

The whole meaning of Christian teaching is precisely that man is *not* alienated from himself by his new relationship to God, but on the contrary, everything that is God's becomes ours in Christ. We discover our true selves in love. To put it more concretely, everything that is God's is our own, *provided that we love.* Here we come to the central point: the question of *love.*

The key problem of humanism is the problem of that au-

thentic love which unites man to man not simply in a sym-
biotic and semiconscious relationship but as person to person
in the authentic freedom of a mutual gift. Here we come to
the question of narcissism, which is closely related to, in fact
inseparable from, alienation. Alienated man is also narcissistic,
because his love is regressive, undeveloped, infantile. It would
be interesting here to examine the possible analogies between
this modern psychological concept and the traditional Christian idea of sin, particularly original sin. They have much in
common. The narcissistic personality is centered on the affirmation of itself and its own limited needs and desires. It
sees other things and persons as real only insofar as they can
be related to these selfish desires.

Psychology and anthropology today teach us that primitive
forms of religion, particularly those which make considerable
use of magic rites, tend to be associated with narcissistic thinking. But we must not place all the blame only on primitive
people. Narcissism remains a problem of enormous magni-
tude, especially in our highly developed modern technological
culture, which abounds in its own hidden forms of magic
thinking, superstition, ritualism. Our sophisticated modern
culture has its taboos, its obsessions, and all that goes into the
formation of the neuroses, individual and collective, which so
often take the place of formal religion in the minds of men.
Erich Fromm even goes so far as to say that much of modern
society and its attitudes can be summed up as highly organized narcissism.

This fascination with the self as a central and sole reality
to be satisfied and catered to in everything is at the root of all
idolatrous forms of religion. Narcissism spontaneously projects
itself onto an idol from which the satisfaction of its desires is
thought to be obtained by magic, by cajoling, by manipulation, or by ruse. The characteristic syndrome of narcissistic
thought ends in this immersion in magic and quasi-omnipo-

tent contemplation of the idol, which is the projection of a selfish and infantile need for love or power.

Though narcissism can be efficiently employed in building up the immense power structures of industrial and military states, it is essentially antihumanistic. Narcissism is hostile to the true development of man's capacity to love. Narcissism alienates man and his society in a slavery to *things*—money, machines, commodities, luxuries, fashions, and pseudoculture. The idolatrous mentality of narcissism produces a fake humanism which cynically deifies man in order to cheat him of his human fulfillment and enslave him to the "rat race" for riches, pleasure, and power. Erich Fromm has pointed out the deadly alliance between the narcissistic mentality of mass-man and the destructive tendencies of a society that grows rich on the prospect of nuclear war.

It must be remembered that collective narcissism is far more mighty and dangerous than the narcissism of the individual. The example of Hitler's Germany is there to remind us to what lengths men will go in order to carry out, to their extreme limit, the rites of a collective self-worship which fills them with a sense of righteousness and complacent satisfaction in the midst of the most shocking injustices and crimes. We find this same narcissism in all the complex military and technological power structures with which millions of men are glad to identify themselves and to which they hand over, without murmur, all moral responsibility for the future of man or for his destruction. The Faustian narcissism and self-idolatry of "post-Christian man" (if the expression be permitted with serious reservations) is, therefore, the greatest single threat to all genuine humanism in our modern world. It is a menace not merely to humanism as a theoretical doctrine but to man himself in the concrete.

One of the things that immediately strike us when we consider this narcissistic and idolatrous cult of collective power is that it is the prime force for the alienation of man today. We also find paradoxically that this force can on occasion appeal to the same philosophical sources which once protested against religion as the opium of the people. We have lived to see that the mythologies of totalistic society (whether dictatorial or plutocratic) are, in fact, a much more powerful "opium" than any of the traditional religions. One can justly entertain serious reservations about the "humanism" of Soviet Russia in the era of Stalin, for example.

The reason for this is not hard to find. In spite of the genial social diagnosis practiced by men like Marx and Feuerbach, and in spite of the theoretical optimism of Marxian eschatology, with its hope that man will finally free himself from alienation and create himself by humanizing his world, we must admit that there are serious limitations.

Like the Hegelian eschatology from which they stem, most modern secular humanisms are concerned with man in the abstract, with the *human species*. It is abstract man who will one day reveal to the world the Absolute made conscious of Itself (Hegel). It is not the free and concrete human person, the man of flesh and blood, but man in general, as a collective totality, who will manifest in himself the latent divinity which is supposed by the Hegelians to be his. Or, for Marx, it is again man, scientific and objective man, who will one day humanize himself and the earth; but Marx had little patience for the claims of the fallible human person, and no interest whatever in such values as love, compassion, mercy, happiness. Thus, it is not difficult for the abstract and scientific doctrines of modern humanism to become means by which the individual person is reduced to subjection to man in the abstract. And as Gabriel Marcel has pointed out, this vast and awful abstractness hovers over the abyss of mass society to bring forth from it the antihumanist and irresponsible monstrosity that is mass-man.

This explains, in part, why modern secular humanisms are so fair and optimistic in theory and so utterly merciless and inhuman in practice. They are so abstract that they easily lend themselves to narcissistic and idolatrous interpretations. It is very easy, in fact, to treat man in the abstract as a narcissistic idol for concrete self-worship. And it is, therefore, very easy to complacently love abstract humanity as the idolatrous projection of self while hating and mercilessly persecuting one's concrete fellow man. Indeed, the unforgiving character of narcissism demands a scapegoat that can "explain" evil and bear the burden of evil on its back. The scapegoat is by definition to be treated with *absolute mercilessness,* for he bears all the evil in the world—he is the source of all evil. Mercilessness is not only permitted, it now becomes a sacred duty. We observe this mercilessness at work in every form of totalism, every form of extreme fanaticism. No matter how much the theoretical doctrines may differ, the practice of all concur in this: love of an abstract good and ideal is taken to justify relentless hatred of a certain group of men in the concrete.

From this we can conclude that the hopes of modern secular and revolutionary eschatology can, in fact, contribute nothing to the building of a new humanism as long as it pretends to attain its ends by the purely objective application of science, without any consideration for living human values as they are incarnate in men of flesh and blood. No humanism has retained the respect for man in his personal and existential actuality to the same extent as Christian humanism. The center of Christian humanism is the idea that God is love, not infinite power. Being Love, God has given himself without reservation to man so that He has become man. Henceforth, by reason of the Incarnation, the love which is also the infinite creative secret of God in his hidden mystery becomes manifest and active, through man, in man's world.

It is man, in Christ, who has the mission of not only mak-

ing himself human but of becoming divine by the gift of the
Spirit of Love. This is not an abstract or contemplative operation only. Love is measured by its activity and its transforming power. Christianity does not teach man to attain an inner
ideal of divine tranquillity and stoic quiet by abstracting himself from material things. It teaches him to give himself to
his brother and to his world in a service of love in which God
will manifest his creative power through men on earth. This
perennial language of Christianity is not bound to any limited
historical world view. It is timeless and points beyond history.
Therefore, it has inexhaustible reserves of creative and transforming energy which can vivify and redirect modern philosophies as it once transformed and elevated the philosophies of
Plato and Aristotle. We have some idea of this, for example,
in the genial thought of Père Teilhard de Chardin in our own
day.

Man is in the midst of the greatest revolution his world has
ever seen. This revolution is not merely political but scientific,
technological, economic, demographic, cultural, spiritual. It
affects every aspect of human life. This revolution in its broad-
est aspects is something that cannot be stopped. The great
question is whether it can truly be directed to ends that are
fully compatible with the authentic dignity and destiny of
man. Science alone, politics alone, economics alone cannot do
this. Still less can the aim be achieved by the power of nuclear
weapons or by guerrilla bands of social revolutionaries. There
must be a full and conscious collaboration of all man's resources of knowledge, technique, and power. But the one hope
of their successful coordination remains the deepest and most
unifying insight that has been granted to man: the Christian
revelation of the unity of all men in the love of God as His
One Son, Jesus Christ.

Christian Humanism in the Nuclear Era

So personalistic was the humanism of the Second Vatican Council that the "Constitution on the Church in the Modern World" might well have been entitled "The Human Person in the Modern World." The whole teaching of the Constitution centers on two things: the value and dignity of the human person in his relation with other men and with God, and the unity of the human family, which is made up of these human persons. It sees the meaning both of the human person and of the whole family of man in the light of the Incarnation. "Only in the Mystery of the Incarnate Word does the mystery of man take on light" (n. 22). It is Christ, in fact, who restores to the human person his divine likeness and freedom, and it is only in Christ that the human family can attain to the peace and unity to which it is called by God. The Council adds: "All this holds true not only for Christians but for all men of good will in whose hearts grace works in an unseen way" (n. 22).

The Church is not identified with any political or economic system, yet she is committed to the common good of all men and to the rights and dignity of the human person. Thus, in her relations with other institutions and in her dealings with men themselves, she will seek above all to encourage every initiative in politics, in culture, in economics, in international relations which will guarantee the greater good of living human persons, while helping the entire human family to live united and in peace. "The Church . . . is not identified in any way with the political community nor bound to any political system. She is at once a sign and a safeguard of the transcendent character of the human person" (n. 76). In other words, the very nature of the Church as a free society of men, united not by mere natural bonds of interest and necessity but by love and grace, is a sign of the transcendent freedom of the human person in Christ, as well as a guarantee of that freedom. For the Church is the place of the encounter of man with Christ and with his fellow man in the Spirit and in agape—or divine reconciliation.

As we go through this Constitution, we find on almost every page some new affirmation of the spiritual dignity of the person, as well as the correlative affirmation that the person attains his full expression only in communal and interpersonal life with others.

The person is defined in terms of freedom, hence in terms of responsibility also: responsibility *to* other persons, responsibility *for* other persons. To put it in concrete terms, the Christian is not only one who seeks the expansion and development of his own individuality and the satisfaction of his most legitimate natural needs but one who recognizes himself responsible for the good of others, for their own temporal fulfillment, and ultimately for their eternal salvation. Hence, the Christian person reaches maturity with the realization that each one of us is indeed his "brother's keeper," and that if men are suffering and dying in Asia or Africa, other men in Europe and America are summoned to self-judgment before the bar of conscience to see whether, in fact, some choice or some neglect on their own part has had a part in this suffering and this dying, which otherwise may seem so strange and remote. For today the whole world is bound tightly together by economic, cultural, and sociological ties which make us all to some extent responsible for what happens to others on the far side of the earth. Man is now not only a social being; his social nature transcends national and regional limits, and whether we like it or not, we must think in terms of one human family, one world.

"One of the salient features of the modern world is the growing interdependence of men one on the other, a development promoted chiefly by modern technical advances. Nevertheless, brotherly dialogue among men does not reach its perfection on the level of technical progress, but on the deeper level of interpersonal relationships. These demand a mutual respect for the full spiritual dignity of the person. Christian revelation contributes greatly to the promotion of this communion between persons, and at the same time leads us to a deeper understanding of the laws of social life which the Creator has written into man's moral and spiritual nature" (n. 23).

"Every day human interdependence grows more tightly drawn and spreads by degrees over the whole earth. As a result the common good, that is, the sum of those conditions of social life which allow social groups and their individual members relatively thorough and ready access to their own fulfillment, today takes on an increasingly universal complexion and consequently involves rights and duties with respect to the whole human race. Every social group must take account of the needs and legitimate aspirations of other groups, and even of the general welfare of the entire human family" (n. 26).

The responsibility of the Christian person, as we see it outlined here, is not confined merely to a realm of inwardness and of pure intentions. It is not just a matter of interior charity and good will. It must also be effective in the context of social action, political life, work, and all the practical choices that affect our relations with others in the family, the city, the nation, and the world. The full development of the Christian person is, then, more than a matter of individual psychological and spiritual adjustment, or even of ascetic perfection. Because man is a son of God, made in the image and likeness of God, he cannot find his true maturity and fulfillment outside a relationship of love with his fellow men. Reconciliation with his fellow man in grace and agape resembles, analogically, the relationship of love between the divine Persons within the Trinity. This is the key to the understanding of Christian social action.

Indeed, the Lord Jesus, when he prayed to the Father, "that all may be one . . . as we are one" (John 17:21–22), opened up vistas closed to human reason, for he implied a certain likeness between the union of the divine Persons and the unity of God's sons in truth and charity. This likeness reveals that man, who is the only creature on earth which God willed for itself, cannot fully find himself except through a sincere gift of himself.

"Man's social nature makes it evident that the progress of the human person and the advance of society itself hinge on one another. For the beginning, the subject and the goal of all social institutions is and must be the human person, which for its part and by its very nature stands completely in need of social life. Since this social life is not something added on to man, through his dealings with others, through reciprocal duties, and through fraternal dialogue he develops all his gifts and is able to rise to his destiny" (nn. 24–5).

The progress of the person and the progress of society therefore go together. Our modern world cannot attain to peace, and to a fully equitable social order, merely by the application of laws which act upon man, so to speak, from outside himself. The transformation of society begins within the person. It begins with the maturing and opening out of personal freedom in relation to other freedoms—in relation to the rest of society. The Christian "giving" that is required of us is a full and intelligent participation in the life of our world, not only on a basis of natural law, but also in the communion and reconciliation of interpersonal love. This means a capacity to be open to others as persons, to desire for others all that we know to be needful for ourselves, all that is required for the full growth and even the temporal happiness of a fully personal existence.

"There is a growing awareness of the exalted dignity proper to the human person, since he stands above all things, and his rights and duties are universal and inviolable. Therefore, there must be made available to all men everything necessary for leading a life truly human, such as food, clothing, and shelter; the right to choose a state of life freely and to found a family, the right to education, to employment, to a good reputation, to respect, to appropriate information, to activity in accord with the upright norm of one's own conscience, to protection of privacy and to rightful freedom, even in matters religious.

"Hence, the social order and its development must invariably work to the benefit of the human person if the disposition of affairs is to be subordinate to the personal realm and not contrariwise, as the Lord indicated when he said that the sabbath was made for man, and not man for the sabbath" (n. 26).

This is the basis for the Council's insistence that Christians must work for a genuine reform and improvement of social institutions and of society itself. Christian charity cannot rest content with a state of affairs in which man is constantly threatened, limited, and deprived of his true capacity to develop as a person.

This social order requires constant improvement. It must

be founded on truth, built on justice, and animated by love; in freedom it should grow every day toward a more humane balance. An improvement in attitudes and abundant changes in society will have to take place if these objectives are to be gained.

The Council left us in no doubt whatever that the duty of Christian participation in the life of the modern world goes further than simply discussing political events and voting at the right time (though this, too, is important). The Christian cannot be fully what he is meant to be in the modern world if he is not in some way interested in *building a better society*, free of war, of racial and social injustice, of poverty, and of discrimination. It is no longer possible to evade this obligation by withdrawing into otherworldly aspirations and pious interiority unconcerned with human and historical problems. On the contrary, eschatological Christian hope is inseparable from an incarnational involvement in the struggle of living and contemporary man.

"Christians, on pilgrimage towards the heavenly city, should seek and think of these things which are above. This duty in no way decreases, rather it increases, the importance of their obligation to work with all men in building a more human world. Indeed, the mystery of the Christian faith furnishes them with an excellent stimulant and aid to fulfill this duty more courageously and especially to uncover the full meaning of this activity, one which gives to human culture its eminent place in the integral vocation of man.

"When man develops the earth by the work of his hands or with the aid of technology, in order that it might bear fruit and become a dwelling worthy of the whole human family, and when he consciously takes part in the life of social groups, he carries out the design of God manifested at the beginning of time, that he should subdue the earth, perfect creation and develop himself. At the same time he obeys the commandment of Christ that he place himself at the service of his brethren" (n. 57).

The right use of scientific means for the improvement of man's social life is seen, by the Council, to be inseparable from the Christian task of preparing the way for the Gospel. Thus, science, far from being regarded with suspicion, is welcomed insofar as it can provide means for the expression of Christian love and prepare the way for the unity of the human family in peace and reconciliation. Therefore, the Church recognizes the values of contemporary culture.

"Among these values are included: scientific study and fidelity towards truth in scientific enquiries, the necessity of working together with others in technical groups, a sense of international solidarity, a clearer awareness of the responsibility of experts to aid and even to protect man, the desire to make the conditions of life more favorable for all, especially for those who are poor in culture or who are deprived of the opportunity to exercise responsibility. All of these provide some preparation for the acceptance of the message of the Gospel—a preparation which can be animated by divine charity through him who has come to save the world" (n. 57).

Recognizing that culture itself is the work of man and is the instrument by which society develops and provides a more favorable atmosphere for the development of the person, the Council reminds the Christian of his duty to work for the spread of education, so that cultural advantages may be made available to everyone without distinction. Then all will be able to share in the work of building a better world.

"The Church recalls to the mind of all that culture is to be subordinated to the integral perfection of the human person, to the good of the community and of the whole society. Therefore it is necessary to develop the human faculties in such a way that there results a growth of the faculty of admiration, of intuition, of contemplation, of making personal

judgment, of developing a religious, moral and social sense"
(n. 59).

"It is now possible to free most of humanity from the
misery of ignorance. Therefore the duty most consonant with
our times, especially for Christians, is that of working dili-
gently for fundamental decisions to be taken in economic and
political affairs, both on the national and international level,
which will everywhere recognize and satisfy the right of all
to a human and social culture in conformity with the dignity
of the human person without any discrimination of race, sex,
nation, religion or social condition. Therefore it is necessary
to provide all with a sufficient quantity of cultural benefits,
especially of those which constitute the so-called fundamental
culture lest very many be prevented from co-operating in the
promotion of the common good in a truly human manner
because of illiteracy and a lack of responsible activity"
(n. 60).

Everywhere in the Constitution we meet the same emphasis. In economic life, what is important is not production for
profit and power but the good of human beings and of the
human family itself. This calls for the transformation and
reform of economic life, since the Council bluntly states that
it does not think that any of the great economic systems now
in power can solve the problem of man.

"Like other areas of social life, the economy of today is
marked by man's increasing domination over nature, by closer
and more intense relationships between citizens, groups, and
countries and their mutual dependence, and by the increased
intervention of the State. At the same time progress in the
methods of production and in the exchange of goods and
services has made the economy an instrument capable of better meeting the intensified needs of the human family.

"Reasons for anxiety, however, are not lacking. Many people, especially in economically advanced areas, seem, as it

were, to be ruled by economics, so that almost their entire personal and social life is permeated with a certain economic way of thinking. Such is true both of nations that favor a collective economy and of others. At the very time when the development of economic life could mitigate social inequalities (provided that it be guided and coordinated in a reasonable and human way), it is often made to embitter them; or, in some places, it even results in a decline of the social status of the underprivileged and in contempt for the poor. While an immense number of people still lack the absolute necessities of life, some, even in less advanced areas, live in luxury or squander wealth. Extravagance and wretchedness exist side by side. While a few enjoy very great power of choice, the majority are deprived of almost all possibility of acting on their own initiative and responsibility, and often subsist in living and working conditions unworthy of the human person.

"Our contemporaries are coming to feel these inequalities with an ever sharper awareness, since they are thoroughly convinced that the ampler technical and economic possibilities which the world of today enjoys can and should correct this unhappy state of affairs. *Hence, many reforms in the socioeconomic realm and a change of mentality and attitude are required of all*" (n. 63; author's italics).

Why does the Church insist on this? Because to her the life and happiness of human persons is more important than economic production and power, which benefits only a few.

"The fundamental finality of this production is not the mere increase of products or profit or control but rather the service of man, and indeed of the whole man with regard for the full range of his material needs and the demands of his intellectual, moral, spiritual, and religious life; this applies to every man whatsoever and to every group of men, of every race and of every part of the world. Consequently, economic activity is to be carried on according to its own methods and laws within the limits of the moral order, so that God's plan for mankind may be realized" (n. 64).

Furthermore, economic development cannot be left to the benign working of economic laws. Improvements can come only through human decision.

"Growth is not to be left solely to a kind of mechanical course of the economic activity of individuals, not to the authority of the government. For this reason, doctrines which obstruct the necessary reforms under the guise of a false liberty, and those which subordinate the basic rights of individual persons and groups to the collective organization of production, must be shown to be erroneous" (n. 65).

Here we see that the Council frankly admitted that progress toward a peaceful world is often, in fact, obstructed by specious ideologies which claim to be the guarantee of human values and of progress. The Council was less concerned with the improvement of ideologies than with the improvement of the living conditions of man. But ideologies which, in fact, keep man in a state of servitude, while claiming to provide him with the best of all possible worlds, must be shown to be filled with absurd self-contradictions, the greatest of which claims that in order to bring peace to the world nations must be ready at any moment for a war of massive extermination.

Turning again to concrete social problems—obviously, working conditions must be such that the worker is not dehumanized or reduced to a level where he functions as something less than a person.

"Since economic activity for the most part implies the associated work of human beings, any way of organizing and directing it which may be detrimental to any working men and women would be wrong and inhuman. It happens too often, however, even in our day, that workers are reduced to the level of being slaves to their own work. This is by no means justified by the so-called economic laws. The entire process of productive work, therefore, must be adapted to the needs of the person and to his way of life, above all to his domestic life, especially in respect to mothers of families, always with due regard for sex and age. The opportunity, moreover, should be granted to workers to unfold their own abilities and personality through the performance of their work. Applying their time and strength to their employment with a due sense of responsibility, they should also all enjoy sufficient rest and leisure to cultivate their familial, cultural, social and religious life. They should also have the opportunity freely to develop the energies and potentialities which perhaps they cannot bring to much fruition in their professional work" (n. 67).

If the right of private property is once again affirmed by the Church, this affirmation is clearly seen in the context of personalism, and it does not exclude a certain necessary socialization in some realms of the economy (see n. 74).

"Since property and other forms of private ownership of external goods contribute to the expression of the personality, and since, moreover, they furnish one an occasion to exercise his function in society and in the economy, it is very important that the access of both individuals and communities to some ownership of external goods be fostered.

"Private property or some ownership of external goods confers on everyone a sphere wholly necessary for the autonomy of the person and the family, and it should be regarded as an extension of human freedom. Lastly, since it adds incentives for carrying on one's function and charge, it constitutes one of the conditions for civil liberties" (n. 71).

However, the basic right of man to own property cannot be adduced to justify the enormous wealth of landowners in certain underdeveloped countries.

"In many underdeveloped regions there are large or even

extensive rural estates which are only slightly cultivated or lie completely idle for the sake of profit, while the majority of the people either are without land or have only very small fields, and, on the other hand, it is evidently urgent to increase the productivity of the fields. Not infrequently those who are hired to work for the landowners or who till a portion of the land as tenants receive a wage or income unworthy of a human being, lack decent housing, and are exploited by middlemen. Deprived of all security, they live under such personal servitude that almost every opportunity of acting on their own initiative and responsibility is denied to them and all advancement in human culture and all sharing in social and political life is forbidden to them. According to the different cases, therefore, reforms are necessary: that income may grow, working conditions should be improved, security in employment increased, and an incentive to working on one's own initiative given. Indeed, insufficiently cultivated estates should be distributed to those who can make these lands fruitful; in this case, the necessary things and means, especially educational aids and the right facilities for cooperative organization, must be supplied. Whenever, nevertheless, the common good requires expropriation, compensation must be reckoned in equity after all the circumstances have been weighed" (n. 71).

We could continue quoting extensively from the Constitution, but by now it is clear that the Council has, on every page, affirmed the rights, the dignities, the duties, and the problems of the human person in modern technological society. We need only add a few lines on political life where, for example, dictatorship is condemned as inhuman (n. 74) and the right to dissent is guaranteed for all, including those who disagree with Christian principles.

"All Christians must be aware of their own specific vocation within the political community. It is for them to give an example by their sense of responsibility and their service of the common good. In this way they are to demonstrate concretely how authority can be compatible with freedom, personal initiative with the solidarity of the whole social organism, and the advantages of unity with fruitful diversity. They must recognize the legitimacy of different opinions with regard to temporal solutions, and respect citizens who, even as a group, defend their points of view by honest methods" (n. 75).

If patriotism is approved, chauvinism is not. The Christian is reminded that his allegiance is first of all to the entire human family, and that he must not appeal to Christian principles in order to justify a patriotism which, in fact, is dangerous or harmful to the universal good of the human race.

"Citizens must cultivate a generous and loyal spirit of patriotism, but without being narrow-minded. This means that they will always direct their attention to the good of the whole human family, united by the different ties which bind together races, people and nations" (n. 75).

This brings us to the crucially important section of the Constitution on modern war. Here the Council frankly declares that a wrongheaded and narrow chauvinism in international relations can be disastrous for the entire human race, since "the whole human family faces an hour of supreme crisis in its advance towards maturity" (n. 77). We are reminded of our obligation to obey natural law, and that blind obedience to civil or military authority will not excuse the man who commits crimes against nature in order to carry out the orders and policies of a state or party. Those who refuse such obedience are praised by the Council.

"Contemplating this melancholy state of humanity, the Council wishes, above all things else, to recall the permanent binding force of universal natural law and its all-embracing principles. Man's conscience itself gives ever more emphatic voice to these principles. Therefore, actions which deliberately conflict with these sane principles, as well as orders commanding such actions, are criminal, and blind obedience cannot excuse those who yield to them. The most infamous among these are actions designed for the methodical extermination of an entire people, nation or ethnic minority. Such actions must be vehemently condemned as horrendous crimes. The courage of those who fearlessly and openly resist those who issue such commands merits supreme commendation" (n. 79).

All Christians are urged to work for peace and to cooperate with those agencies and officials who are trying to bring about a peaceful settlement of international disputes, to end the arms race, and to prepare for a future international order in which war will be outlawed. Naturally, conflict will always exist, but it should be limited and, if possible, entirely prevented by international authority from erupting into violence.

"On the subject of war, quite a large number of nations have subscribed to international agreements aimed at making military activity and its consequences less inhuman. Their stipulations deal with such matters as the treatment of wounded soldiers and prisoners. Agreements of this sort must be honored. Indeed they should be improved upon so that the frightfulness of war can be better and more workably held in check. All men, especially government officials and experts in these matters, are bound to do everything they can to effect these improvements" (n. 79).

The Council does not deny the legitimate right of a nation to self-defense, particularly where no strong international police authority exists to prevent war. But the Council refused to accede to the desire of some bishops and to *approve* of nuclear stockpiles used as a deterrent. While refraining from deciding this question by a clear condemnation of the nuclear deterrent as such (though it did condemn massive and indiscriminate destruction), the Council simply stated that this could never guarantee a "sure and authentic peace."

The Council clearly maintained that force and violence would never be a firm basis for peace, but it did leave a word of special approval for those who seek non-violent ways of conflict resolution.

"We cannot fail to praise those who renounce the use of violence in the vindication of their rights and who resort to methods of defense which are otherwise available to weaker parties too, provided this can be done without injury to the rights and duties of others or of the community itself.

"Insofar as men are sinful, the threat of war hangs over them, and hang over them it will until the return of Christ. But insofar as men vanquish sin by a union of love, they will vanquish violence as well and make these words come true: 'They shall turn their swords into ploughshares, and their spears into sickles. Nation shall not lift up sword against nation, neither shall they learn war any more' (Isaiah 2.4)" (n. 78).

When non-violence is commended by the Constitution, it is understood that this commendation applies to true non-violence as a most serious form of spiritual and political discipline: the non-violence that was practiced and brought to perfection by Gandhi and has also been used with discipline and effect by Martin Luther King and the Negro civil-rights demonstrators in the South of the United States. On the other hand, not everything that is publicized as "non-violence" in the mass media comes up to the standards demanded by the teachings of Gandhi. The Council's approval does not extend to forms of protest which are merely *substitutes for violence,* and which often contain elements of psychological and emotional violence which are incompatible with true non-violence. Such protests are dismissed by Gandhi as the "non-violence of the weak," that is to say, simple expedients adopted by people who know that violence would be ineffective and who wish to express their hatred, spite, and contempt in some other way. True non-violence demands not only self-control, sincere devotion to the common good, including that of the adversary, but also, according to Gandhi, belief in God.

In any event, whether or not the Christian submits to the discipline of non-violent resistance to force, he has a clear obligation to work for world peace according to the measure of his ability. In so doing he is cooperating with Christ, the Prince of Peace, and living up to the demands of the Gospel.

"Consequently, as it points out the authentic and noblest meaning of peace and condemns the frightfulness of war, the Council wishes passionately to summon Christians to co-operate, under the help of Christ, the author of peace, with all men in securing among themselves a peace based on justice and love and in setting up the instruments of peace.

"Peace is not merely the absence of war; nor can it be re-duced solely to the maintenance of a balance of power be-tween enemies; nor is it brought about by dictatorship. Peace results from that order structured into human society by its divine Founder, and actualized by men as they thirst after ever greater justice. The common good of humanity finds its ultimate meaning in the eternal law. But since the concrete demands of this common good are constantly changing as time goes on, peace is never attained once and for all, but must be built up ceaselessly. Moreover, since the human will is unsteady and wounded by sin, the achievement of peace requires a constant mastering of passions and the vigilance of lawful authority.

"But this is not enough. This peace on earth cannot be obtained unless personal well-being is safeguarded and men freely and trustingly share with one another the riches of their inner spirits and their talents. A firm determination to respect other men and peoples and their dignity, as well as the studied practice of brotherhood, are absolutely necessary for the establishment of peace. Hence peace is likewise the fruit of love, which goes beyond what justice can provide" (nn. 77–8).

The question of conscientious objection was discussed in the Council and a rather strong affirmation of the religious and evangelical character of conscientious objection was proposed to the Schema. This did not appear in the final version, but nevertheless the Constitution approved of conscientious objection by explicitly recommending laws to provide for conscientious objectors. The Council distinguished between conscientious objection and negative, anarchistic protest by suggesting that objectors should offer an alternative peaceful service in society.

"Moreover, it seems right that laws make humane provisions for the case of those who for reasons of conscience refuse to bear arms, provided however that they agree to serve the human community in some other way" (n. 79).

All this is to be seen against the background of the Council's condemnation of total war in the clearest and most unequivocal language.

"The horror and perversity of war is immensely magnified by the addition of scientific weapons. For acts of war involving these weapons can inflict massive and indiscriminate destruction, thus going far beyond the bounds of legitimate defense. Indeed, if the kind of instruments which can now be found in the armories of the great nations were to be employed to their fullest, an almost total and altogether reciprocal slaughter of each side by the other would follow, not to mention the widespread devastation that would take place in the world and the deadly after-effects that would be spawned by the use of weapons of this kind.

"With these truths in mind, this most holy Synod makes its own the condemnations of total war already pronounced by recent popes, and issues the following declaration.

"Any act of war aimed indiscriminately at the destruction of entire cities or extensive areas along with their population is a crime against God and man himself. It merits unequivocal and unhesitating condemnation.

"The unique hazard of modern warfare consists in this: it provides those who possess modern scientific weapons with a kind of occasion for perpetrating just such abominations; moreover, through a certain inexorable chain of events, it can catapult men into the most atrocious decisions. That such may never truly happen in the future, the bishops of the whole world gathered together, beg all men, especially government officials and military leaders, to give unremitting thought to their gigantic responsibility before God and the entire human race" (n. 80).

Here, above all, a whole new attitude toward war is demanded. The Council solemnly affirmed that all men must take seriously and personally the obligation incumbent on the entire human race to abolish war.

"All these considerations compel us to undertake an evaluation of war with an entirely new attitude. The men of our time must realize that they will have to give a somber reckoning of their deeds of war for the course of the future which will depend greatly on the decisions they make today" (n. 80).

Hence the Council, to the chagrin of a few bishops, refused to bless the present dangerous and absurd situation, which depends precariously on deterrence. This cannot be tolerated as normal. As soon as possible, other and safer means of preventing war must be found.

"Whatever be the facts about this method of deterrence, men should be convinced that the arms race in which an already considerable number of countries are engaged is not a safe way to preserve a steady peace, nor is the so-called balance resulting from this race a sure and authentic peace. Rather than being eliminated thereby, the causes of war are in danger of being gradually aggravated. While extravagant sums are being spent for the furnishing of ever new weapons, an adequate remedy cannot be provided for the multiple miseries afflicting the whole modern world. Disagreements between nations are not really and radically healed; on the contrary, they spread the infection to other parts of the earth. New approaches based on reformed attitudes must be taken to remove this trap and to emancipate the world from its crushing anxiety through the restoration of genuine peace.

"Therefore, we say it again: the arms race is an utterly treacherous trap for humanity, and one which ensnares the poor to an intolerable degree. It is much to be feared that if this race persists, it will eventually spawn all the lethal ruin whose path it is now making ready" (n. 81).

This rapid glance at the "Constitution on the Church in the Modern World" shows us a clearly optimistic, positive, and open approach to modern man. Here is a deeply traditional Christian humanism which is willing and able to collaborate with modern science and technology in building a new world for man. In this new world, modern technology will (if it is used in man's true interests) enable man to live at last in relative peace, with a high degree of temporal comfort, and with an amount of leisure which he can use to great advantage, provided that he knows how. But the Church is not assuming that all this will come about automatically, and the Constitution is not saying that science alone will bring this new utopia as though by magic.

Nor does the optimism of the Constitution anywhere imply a naïve satisfaction with our present social situation. Far from imparting a blessing to any particular social or economic system, the Council clearly understands that our present social institutions are powerless to resolve our crisis and indeed are to some extent responsible for it. Hence, the Constitution says clearly that unless we change our present direction, and unless the structure of our technological society is radically developed and improved, we cannot expect the hopes of humanism, Christian or otherwise, to be realized. On the contrary, though avoiding pessimism, the Constitution does recognize that we are in a state of grave crisis and does foresee the possibility of disaster—a possibility which no one in his right mind can ignore.

The Universe as Epiphany

AUTHOR'S NOTE: The following is an attempt at a positive and sympathetic appreciation of a much discussed writer who is certainly not without confusions and limitations. This essay is concerned with the spiritual implications of his scientific-religious mystique. In this field of practical deductions the thought of Teilhard de Chardin is less debatable than are his well-known theses on evolutionism.

The French Jesuit scientist Father Pierre Teilhard de Chardin has become famous, since his death in 1955, as the author of a remarkable and much discussed volume, *The Phenomenon of Man*. Speaking at the same time with the objectivity of a scientist and with the fervor of a contemplative, the Jesuit paleontologist was perhaps the first Catholic thinker who successfully incorporated the modern scientific world view into an authentically Christian and even mystical philosophy of life. In order to do so, he did not fear to embrace a mitigated evolutionism which is not alien to religion, but is, in fact, incomprehensible without it. It was clear that Teilhard de Chardin was too great and profound a thinker to be content with the superficial rationalizing which has so often attempted to "reconcile science and religion" and has ended only in an absurd compromise. Certainly in his own mind the conflict, if it had ever existed at all, was completely resolved in a higher and contemplative wisdom. However, the wisdom of Teilhard de Chardin, presented in somewhat new and unfamiliar terms, and introduced by Sir Julian Huxley, could not fail to disturb some members of the Catholic hierarchy, and it has yet to be accepted without reservations.

The Phenomenon of Man was Teilhard de Chardin's last and most mature work. The controversy which surrounded its appearance may, perhaps, have had something to do with the publication of a much earlier book, *The Divine Milieu,* which will enable students to appreciate the profoundly Christian depths of Teilhard's scientific and religious synthesis. My purpose here is simply to evaluate *The Divine Milieu* as a book in its own right, standing by itself, leaving to others the detailed study of its relationship to the more profound and scientific vision of the author's final years.

This earlier volume, a fervent and inspired meditation on the place of the created world in the spiritual life, was written in 1926, when Teilhard de Chardin was working as a member of a scientific expedition in China. It is certainly not controversial to the same degree as *The Phenomenon of Man,* though it is sufficiently vital and independent in its thought to trouble minds that fear the very shadow of originality as somehow "dangerous." But I do not think any responsible theologian who takes the trouble to interpret the author's true meaning will find in it anything he can possibly condemn. In any case, we have here a work of entirely different scope, not speculative but practical, and one which will certainly exert a healthy force on the lives of those who read it intelligently.

I The Problem of Christian Humanism

There can be no question that Christianity has been very seriously challenged in our time, and not everyone who has challenged it has been acting out of malice or bad faith, as

Christians sometimes seem to believe. It has been seriously asked whether or not the Christian view of the cosmos could possibly survive Einstein and the exploration of outer space— as if an "unlimited" and expanding complex of universes were too "big" to allow for a God! A curious anxiety, which fails to grasp the metaphysical concept of transcendence! At the same time, in the anguished confusion of modern life, in which man is struggling without too much success to "find himself" in his new loneliness and build himself a society commensurate with his newfound opportunities, it has repeatedly been asked whether or not Christian moral and spiritual perspectives did not, in fact, diminish and frustrate man's true development as man. Does not Christianity confine man within the limitations of a narrow set of myths which forbid him to effect a creative adjustment to the reality around him? In a word, Teilhard de Chardin starts out by confronting the accusation that as long as we remain Christians we are doomed to obscurantism, retrogression, reaction, and flight from reality; that as long as we are Christian we are bound by the very nature of our spirituality to *react against* every honest effort to make full use of natural forces and to create a "better world."

What is the basis of these accusations? Teilhard de Chardin thinks that they manage to borrow some foundation of truth from the actual behavior of many Christians who are to some extent spiritually crippled by the lack of a truly Christian moral perspective. For too many Christians, in fact, Christianity is an entirely negative religion which seems to prescribe a complete alienation from life, from human values, and from the world, if one is to hope for union with God. The doctrine of the Cross, diminished and distorted because it is separated from the mystery of the Resurrection, becomes a doctrine of death and not of life. The Christian is, then, supposed to pass through life passive, inert, and indifferent. He is not called upon to react creatively to the challenges, the obstacles, and the opportunities of life, but merely to *submit* without understanding to a blind force which he calls "the will of God." This will does not enter into his life as a creative or loving power, but merely as an inexorable and meaningless authoritarian pressure, a stoic necessity. For such a Christian, all material things are either evil or dangerous, and even if one admits that the world is "good," it must nevertheless be ignored and rejected because its goodness is only a snare that will captivate us and keep us from seeing God. The only true spiritual development possible to man is a one-sided ascetic withdrawal from material things into a purely immaterial realm of ideas and angelic beings. The world is, then, an obstacle. Any desire to change the status quo is satanic pride. Things are just what God has willed them to be, and his will is static, conservative, since "He cannot change." Any attempt to see the world and history as dynamic developments in which man's freedom plays a constructive and, indeed, essential part would be, according to this view, a dangerously radical temptation.

Such is the false notion of a *disincarnate* or *disembodied* Christianity which, in fact, is not Christian at all, for he who says "Christianity" says "Incarnation." This is what in practice serves as "spirituality" for many Christians.

Hence, the modern world is insulated against Christianity by the inveterate suspicion that Christianity seeks to make man *inhuman*, that Christian asceticism is nothing else than the denial and repression of all that is vital and human in man precisely because it is vital. In a word, Christianity empties human life of meaning in order to draw the Christian aside from the normal activities of life and make him concentrate on another "purely spiritual" world which has nothing to do with the present one and with its multiple responsibilities. Christianity is, therefore, nothing but an evasion. And so Christian humanism is only a word: it cannot possibly represent a genuine reality.

II The Divine Center

Such objections to Christianity occur only to those who have no real grasp of the meaning of the Christian revelation, because they see it only as a set of abstract doctrinal propositions instead of experiencing it as a unified life "in Christ." The true Christian view of the universe obviously does not postulate the existence of an anthropomorphic "watchmaker" existing spatially "outside" and "above" a universe contained within rigidly fixed limits. This would be a childish notion of divine transcendence which is a metaphysical note of the God Who is at the same time infinitely "other than" all that we know as being, and yet immanent in everything that exists, so that He is, in fact, the "center" of every being and of all reality, including material reality. The divine center, to which all things point, toward which they all aspire, is at the same time a "divine milieu" which surrounds, sustains, and embraces them all together in harmony and in unity. All beings are "held" from within by their gravitation to the divine center (in the metaphysical heart of their own being) and moved from without by the divine power of the milieu which God has set all about them. The destiny of all beings is brought into a single focus and aimed in the same direction by the wisdom of God, and man's vocation is incomprehensible unless it is seen precisely in relation to the world of matter into which he is born and in which he must work out "his salvation." For man is "in the world" not, as Plato believed, as a spirit "fallen" from the immaterial into the prison of matter but as a son of God called to cooperate with his Father in the work of ruling and of redeeming the material universe along with himself.

The perspectives of Teilhard de Chardin are those of St. Paul, *the recapitulation of all things in Christ*. The radiant focus of all reality is not only the Divine Being but God Incarnate, Jesus Christ. The spirit of man exists for Christ. But material things exist for man in Christ. Not only should they not be obstacles to our union with Christ, but they are indispensable for our service and knowledge of Christ. The Lord not only manifests Himself to us in material Creation, He even gives Himself to us in matter sanctified and sacramentalized by the power He has handed over to His priesthood and His Church. It is important to notice the sublimely eucharistic heart of the spirituality of Teilhard de Chardin. Christ comes into the world giving Himself to man: and man, in return, receiving Christ in and with the world, redeems material creation by using it in the service of Christ. Now Christ, in Teilhard de Chardin, is not merely the Risen Lord dwelling in heaven; he is also and above all the Mystical Christ, living and working in mankind. Man's vocation in life is, therefore, no evasion from the world: it is to be "in the world" but not "of the world" by "being Christ" in the world and thus offering the whole world to the Father in union with Christ. Nor is this "offering" a purely hieratic and ritual act. Our everyday lives are meant to prolong our daily participation in the Eucharist and to bear the fruits of that participation by a renewed and intensified communion with Christ in His creation. This communion is not a matter of *work*. The heart of the spirituality of Teilhard de Chardin is, then, his idea of man's redemption of his world by creative activity in union with Christ. The Christian is called to help recapitulate all things in Christ, not only by prayer, liturgy, and meditation, but above all by action. Not that Teilhard de Chardin is an "activist" who prefers action to prayer and despises the "interior life," but rather that he sees far beyond the supposed contradiction between action and contemplation, realizing clearly that one cannot exist without the other; that action without this mystical and contemplative dimension is sterile and absurd, while contemplation that has no impact on man's world and on his daily life is a puerile evasion.

"Let us establish ourselves," he says, "in the divine milieu. There we shall find ourselves where the soul is most deep and where matter is most dense. There we shall discover with the confluence of all beauties, the ultra-vital, the ultra-sensitive, the ultra-active point of the universe. And at the same time, we shall feel the *plenitude* of our powers of action and adoration effortlessly ordered within our deepest selves."

III Creativity

All Christian life is meant to be at the same time profoundly contemplative and rich in active work. This must not be mistaken for a kind of semipelagian productivism which is obsessed with visible results and enamored of technological prowess. It is true that we are called to create a better world. But we are first of all called to a more immediate and exalted task: that of creating our own lives. In doing this, we act as co-workers with God. We take our place in the great work of mankind, since in effect the creation of our own destiny, in God, is impossible in pure isolation. Each one of us works out his own destiny in inseparable union with all those others with whom God has willed us to live. We share with one another the creative work of living in the world. And it is through our struggle with material reality, with nature, that we help one another create at the same time our own destiny and a new world for our descendants. This work of man, which is his peculiar and inescapable vocation, is a prolongation of the creative work of God Himself. Failure to measure up to this challenge and to meet this creative responsibility is to fail in that response to life which is required of us by the will of our Father and Creator.

This active response, this fidelity to life itself and to God Who gives Himself to us through our daily contacts with the material world, is the first and most essential duty of man. For it is only in this way that he really fulfills in his deeds (rather than in words) the command to adore God his Creator. Without this active response, there is no real love for God, no real doing of His will. Teilhard de Chardin very rightly draws attention to the falsity of those pseudoascetic ideals which undermine the Christian spirit along with man's human vitality by tempting man to escape this basic responsibility. He is especially critical of the false resignation, the passivity which pretends to obey by "accepting" when, in fact, it simply rejects the realities of life and evades the tasks which life imposes. One of the most formal obligations of the Christian is to struggle against evil, whether it be moral or physical. The Christian can only resign himself passively to the acceptance of evil when it is quite clear that he is powerless to do anything about it. Hence, it is an utterly false Christianity which preaches the supine acceptance of social injustice, ignorance, impossible working conditions, and war as though it were virtue to "take" all this and "offer it up" without even attempting to change anything. His view of Christian virtue is far from the stoic resignation which accepts decrees of "fate" with a carefully cultivated insensibility. He has no patience with a concept of "purity of intention" which is completely divorced from the action to be performed. How can we have a really "pure" intention to do the will of God, if, in fact, we are completely indifferent to the quality of the work performed in response to the demands of life which are in fact God's own demand? The genuine "purity" of Christian action will, indeed, teach man to work without undue concern for the results of his efforts, but will not make him utterly indifferent to the work itself, since he will see clearly that his work is a communion with God his Creator, in which he not only unites himself to God but also "saves" and transforms the material world "in Christ."

So, says our author, "whatever our human function may be, whether artist or working man or scholar we can, if we are Christians, speed toward the object of our work as though toward an outlet open for the supreme fulfillment of our beings. Indeed, without exaggeration or excess in thought or expression—but simply by confronting the most fundamental truths of our faith and of experience—we are led to the following observation: God is inexhaustibly attainable in the *totality* of our action. And this prodigy of divinisation is only comparable to the gentleness with which the metamorphosis is accomplished, without disturbing in any way the perfection and unity of human endeavor."

VI "The Divinisation of Passivities"

If Teilhard de Chardin had been an activist or a pelagian (and no doubt he will be called both), he could never have written the crucial and exciting chapter on what he calls man's "passivities." An activist has no respect for anything that is not under the direct control of reason and will. He exploits his powers for the sake of action itself, which is, to him, a refuge or an end. Activism enables him to forget that the greater part of his being and of his life is obscure, hidden, and beyond his control.

Teilhard de Chardin is deeply concerned with the passive realm in man—first with the passivities of growth, then above all with those of diminishment, which include all possible obstacles, frustrations, and evils, even death itself. From all these we not only can but must draw positive spiritual fruit. Life must not be simply accepted or undergone: it must be *lived*. Evil itself must be not merely "borne" but resisted, used, turned to good account. In all our passivities, whether of growth or of diminishment, and even in the ultimate passivity of death, in which our whole being disintegrates, man can and must enter into communion with Christ.

Speaking of the passivities of growth, Teilhard de Chardin gives free play to his admirable poetic gifts in one of his many soliloquies which echo St. Augustine and St. Anselm and situate him in the great tradition of Christian contemplation. "O God, Whose call precedes the very first of our movements, grant me the desire to desire being—that by means of that divine thirst which is Your gift, the access to the great waters may open wide within me. Do not deprive me of the sacred taste for being, that primordial energy, that initial point of support: *Spiritu Principali confirma me.*" We should not merely "be" but experience our being in its depths by freely willing to be, by responding to the gift of being that comes to us from God within us, by attaining to a "fontal communion" with Him as the source and center of our life. No finer and more contemplative page has been written in our century. And it gives us the key to the mysticism of Teilhard de Chardin, showing us that in this above all he is an authentic witness to Christian tradition.

The passivities of diminishment are harder to handle. We need much greater faith to see God coming to us in sickness, in death, and even in the errors and mistakes of our life. Here, too, the rather novel terminology of Teilhard de Chardin must not blind the Catholic reader to the fact that we have here a statement of the deepest and most traditional of Christian truths, unobscured and untainted by any false stoicism or any Manichaean passivity toward evil. On the contrary, if the Christian "accepts" evil into his life with stoic indifference, or still worse remains unconcerned with the crises of society and of mankind, he cannot enter into communion with Christ. "If he is to practice to the full the perfection of Christianity, the Christian must not falter in his duty to resist evil." Why? Because evil is not something that God wills him to "undergo" with patience and negative resignation. God does not simply ask man to suffer. Suffering is an evil. If evil comes into our life, it is in order that we may grow and give glory to God by cooperating with him in resisting it.

Christ's command "resist not evil" is no objection against this. On the contrary, the resistance forbidden by Christ is the simple, selfish instinct to repel suffering and to escape it. The Christian is bound to "overcome evil with good" and hence to resist it in a higher and more perfect sense: consciously and freely working to bring out of evil that good which is willed by God. Clearly this is a much more healthy and fruitful concept of Christian patience than the negative one which asks us to bear every stupid injustice, to obey and keep our mouths shut because, for some unknown reason which is none of our business, God has decreed that we must be crushed under some burden of suffering.

V "For Those Who Love the World"

There is no better description of Teilhard de Chardin than this sentence of his, which contains his whole attitude and his deeply Christian love for God's creation: "The man with a passionate sense of the divine milieu *cannot bear to find things around him obscure, tepid and empty which should be full and vibrant with God.*" That is why he roundly asserts that he loves the world instead of hating it. Is this wrong? On the contrary, the flyleaf of the book bears four Latin words from

the Gospel of St. John: *Sic Deus dilexit mundum,* "God so
loved the world . . ." and the book is dedicated to "those
who Love the World."

Like so many other key terms in the New Testament, the
"world" is used in two senses. One which is to be "hated"
and the other to be "loved." Now it is precisely the "world"
that is "empty, obscure, and without God" that is to be
hated. But the difference between the two worlds *depends on
us.* It is we who leave the world as empty as we find it, or
we who, on the contrary, fill the world with divine meaning.
To be sure, God is "in the world," but He is hidden in it,
and unless we by our own free action and fidelity to His
mysterious purposes cooperate with Him, His epiphany in the
world, His manifestation of Himself cannot be perfectly realized. Certainly He will see Himself in the world, but the
point is that He wants to be seen and received in another
way: He wants to reveal Himself to man in a "new Creation." He wants to be received not simply by individual men
with prophetic power or poetic wisdom but by *all men.* When
mankind as a whole, and all individual men, open their arms
to God, then He will appear to them in their world and in
themselves. It will be a "new world" and they will be "new
men." But this "Parousia" (which, as Teilhard declares, most
Christians have "ceased to expect") is not possible without
the cooperation of the saints. Hence, it is the duty of the
Christian to love the world by doing all in his power, with
the help of God's grace and fidelity to the demands of the
divine will in his everyday life, to "redeem" the whole world,
to transform and consecrate it to the divinizing power of the
Spirit of Christ.

What Teilhard de Chardin most laments is that Christians
have apparently abandoned this sublime expectation, which
is the very essence of the Gospel. They have turned aside into
tiny, obscure, and stuffy individual ways of salvation which

are devoid of ultimate meaning except that they make each one a participant in everlasting bliss and above all help each one to escape everlasting torment. But too many Christians have refused to sympathize with the genuine, sincere, though sometimes misguided hopes of the men of their time. Teilhard declares without ambiguity that "we should share those aspirations, in essence religious, which make the men of today feel strongly the immensity of the world, the greatness of the mind, and the sacred value of every new truth." Not for the sake of novelty of human progress, but because such dynamic developments are clues to the mystery of God's will and of His action in history, and because by corresponding to the graces and appeals of our own time we can and must manifest our "operative expectation of the Parousia." To act otherwise, even for the most laudable of motives, is an implicit confession of infidelity, of distrust in God, and even of despair.

The risks that Teilhard de Chardin demands of us are, therefore, in no way the perils of modernism, of naturalism, of scientism. On the contrary, this scientist and priest is speaking above all as a mystic. That is to say, he speaks the language of Patristic wisdom, which is basically contemplative and mystical rather than technical and exact. He is a scientist who writes as a poet, and writes for prospective saints, rather than for his fellow scientists as such. He is above all a priest, and the deepest concern of his book is the concern of a priest, a minister of Christ, one *sent by Christ,* with a mission to "love the world" as Christ has loved it, and therefore to seek and to find in it all the good which is hidden there and which Christ died on the Cross to recover. Only in these priestly and eucharistic perspectives can we really understand the great work of Teilhard de Chardin and his profound sympathy for everything human and for every legitimate aspiration of modern man, even though that man may sometimes be a misguided and errant thinker, a heretic, an atheist.

"The greater man becomes, the more humanity becomes united, with the consciousness of and mastery of its potentialities, the more beautiful creation will be, the more perfect adoration will become, and the more Christ will find, for mystical extensions, a body worthy of Resurrection."

Teilhard's Gamble

It is neither difficult nor unusual to contrast the optimism of Teilhard de Chardin with the pessimism of Pascal, yet the two have much in common. Not only did they both come from the central mountains of France, the Auvergne; not only were they both scientists who reacted as Christians to the scientific revolutions of their times; they also constructed apologetic syntheses which they felt would revive the faith and reinvigorate the Christian life of their contemporaries. Both were creative spirits as adventurous as they were gifted. Both reacted forcefully against the dead inertia of merely conventional Christianity. Both were controversial figures, venerated by some as prophets and mystics, execrated by others as heretics or religious cranks. Both recognized the urgent need for a restatement of familiar truths in a language viable for a new religious consciousness. Of course, Pascal did not, like Teilhard, create a whole new vocabulary. He spoke the language of his time. Confronting the "infinite spaces" opened up by the discoveries of Copernicus and Galileo, the vastness of a universe in which tiny man seemed lost, he urged the Christian to gamble with his existential freedom and make the wager of faith in the solitude of his own heart. Teilhard, confronting the ongoing and open-ended process of evolution—adduced by some as a final proof of the unimportance of man—proceeded to put man right back into the center of the picture. In each case, the Christian answer to a quantitative conception of man in the world was a reaffirmation of value and quality. For Pascal this centered in the personal freedom of the individual believer; for Teilhard in the collective freedom of persons committed together to a common task of "planetization."

Even though Teilhard seeks to base his cosmic and "Christic" humanism on scientific evidence, it is ultimately a wager something like Pascal's. Teilhard does not reach his grandiose conclusions by sheer induction: on the contrary, it all starts with an intuitive and global illumination, elaborated into a scientific mystique. Pascal gambles on the individual's relation with Christ in faith. In other words, he bets that since man needs a Savior he must really have one. Teilhard gambles on God's need for man, since without man God's creative plan cannot be fulfilled. Without man, God's face cannot be fully manifest in his evolving creation. Man has an inescapable inner need to be the locus of the divine epiphany, because in him the universe has at last become conscious of itself. And "the universe by structural necessity cannot disappoint the consciousness it produces."

The whole structure of Teilhard's "religious thought," which is the subject of Henri De Lubac's book about him (*The Religion of Teilhard de Chardin*), is based on this contention that evolution has made man once again the center of the universe, not spatially, not metaphysically, but in Teilhard's word, "structurally." "Man is the hub of the universe . . . the structural key to the universe." Hence, for Teilhard it is not only religion but science itself which declares that "man is the key and not an anomaly" in the world of evolution. For "man is the greatest telluric and biological event on our planet" and "the supreme achievement of the organizing power of the cosmos." Consequently, man is "the key to the whole science of nature" and the "solution of everything that we can know." This is the principal challenge of Teilhard to the thought of his time, and it is a challenge which, implemented by a cosmic and incarnational mystique, is directed against scientific positivism more than against the traditional theology of the Church. Indeed, one would have expected the scientists to dismiss Teilhard's thesis as reactionary even more emphatically than the theologians who fought it as revolutionary. But scientists were on the whole more friendly to Teilhard than theologians.

It is certainly true that the immense popularity of Teilhard is due in part to the censorship which strove to keep his writings out of reach. The censors themselves did more than anyone else to confer upon Teilhard the aura of charismatic authority which he enjoys among those who are fed up with indexes and inquisitions. And now Teilhard is doubly fortunate in having one of the best theologians of his Order, Father Henri De Lubac—who also bears a few scars from the days of *Humani Generis*—to vouch for the perfect orthodoxy of his doctrine, at least in its basic orientation.

The title of the translation, *The Religion of Teilhard de Chardin,* is perhaps unfortunate. "Religion" in English does not properly render *"pensée religieuse."* Why does De Lubac announce his intention to study the "religious thinking" rather than the "theology" of Teilhard? De Lubac is all the more ready to admit that Teilhard is "not a theologian or a philosopher," because he considers this in some respects an advantage. Teilhard was, like Pascal, the kind of religious genius who fell outside the ordinary categories and who would have been hampered in his creative originality if he had had to fit his thought into strictly technical limitations. True, this had disadvantages also. Teilhard's thought is in some respects undisciplined and confusing to the theologian, open to perhaps misinterpretation by the layman. His new language is not always felicitous, and is sometimes tedious, sometimes

even comic, as De Lubac freely admits. Nevertheless, Teilhard is a genius, a unique, indeed a providential combination
of the scientist and the mystic.

De Lubac accepts without question that Teilhard is a true
mystic, that his basic intuitions are entirely and profoundly
Catholic, and that his shortcomings are purely incidental matters of expression.

De Lubac has brought to bear the full force of his scholar-
ship upon the task of showing that all Teilhard's statements
can be understood in a perfectly traditional sense, or at least
in a way that does not contradict Catholic tradition. As an
expert in Origen and the Greek Fathers, De Lubac indicates
the deep affinities between Teilhard and the Alexandrians.
One regrets that he does so only in passing: this is a theme
which could be profitably developed. But De Lubac is concerned with the more urgent business of showing that there
is nothing suspect in Teilhard. He does so fairly successfully,
insofar as he concentrates on the "religious thinking" of Teilhard, especially in its practical consequences for the Christian
life. This book is, in reality, a summa of Teilhard's spiritual
doctrine: his teaching on the ascetic and mystical life in the
context of his evolutionary and incarnational cosmogony. This
teaching is centered in one of Teilhard's most indisputably
classic works, *The Divine Milieu,* but De Lubac also draws
on many other documents, including much that has not appeared in print. The only sources not quoted are the "most
intimate" letters, which reflect Teilhard's difficulties with his
superiors and which remain classified. (De Lubac intimates
that they will only prove more thoroughly Teilhard's fidelity
to traditional ideas of religious obedience.)

The religious thought and spiritual doctrine of Teilhard
center in his theory of man's present task on earth. According
to his estimate of the evolutionary process, man is now at a

point of decisive and revolutionary change: a point as crucial as that when, a million-odd years ago, human consciousness broke through and man ceased to be an ape. But the point at which we now stand—the point at which we are about to enter a "collective Christic superconsciousness" and a higher civilization—has not only a human but also a decisively spiritual character: one might almost say it is a mystical and eschatological event, except that this does not correspond accurately to Teilhard's way of speaking. "History is about to fuse with the transcendent," Teilhard would say. Cosmic evolution is reaching the point of "convergence" upon a "personal center." In fact, we are already in year eleven of the Noosphere! (I don't know how seriously we are meant to take Teilhard's assertion that the Noosphere would begin in the Geophysical year of 1957.) We are entering upon the "planetization of mankind." Man is ready for "totalization" in a collective task. He must use science and technology to humanize and spiritualize matter, thus preparing it for the advent of Christ. "The whole process of hominization is simply a preparation of the final Parousia." We are now called to "fundamental oneness," to a collaborative task, to "master the universe, to examine its secrets, to become one with all men in a higher community in which conscious minds will be illuminated by convergence in which consciousness will have freed or penetrated all matter." Teilhardian man is, then, not lost and alone in a threatening cosmos, but at home in a happy world which is entirely his and which Christ is waiting for him to transform. "Christ is waiting to reappear until the human collectivity has become capable . . . of receiving from him its supernatural consummation." Teilhardian man is one who gambles entirely on the future. He is a "pilgrim of the future," and he refuses to be diverted from his pilgrimage even by the H bomb, which Teilhard found very inspiring: it was only a manifestation of the "dawn of a Christic neo-energy."

Clearly, the Teilhardian wager is as much a gamble as Pascal's. Perhaps it is more of a gamble. Pascal's existential thinking confines itself to the area of individual freedom, and the individual can decide his own spiritual destiny! Teilhard has hocked everything and bet it on the human species. He has done so at a moment when the odds seem somewhat long against the kind of runaway win he anticipates. Teilhard does not seem to notice the wounds of mendacity and hatred which have been inexorably deepened in man by his practice of technological warfare, totalitarianism, and genocide. Certainly we can sympathize with the admirable innocence of his hope. But is it, as he believes, and as De Lubac concurs, a completely valid extrapolation of Bible eschatology? Is Teilhard so convinced that he bet right that he obstinately refuses to see any possibility of losing? At times, the Teilhardian synthesis seems to demand nothing short of blind faith in predetermined evolutionary success: the Noosphere is here, the superconsciousness is dawning and—this De Lubac neglected to add—the armies of Mao marching in Peking in 1951 were seen by Teilhard as the vanguard of a new humanity. Everything is already in the bag. You can't lose: "It would be easier to halt the turning of the earth than it would be to prevent the totalization of mankind." Also, one is tempted to wonder: Is this "totalization," this "superconsciousness," "this complete co-reflection" the Mystical Christ or the Dictatorship of the Proletariat?

There are moments when Teilhard does not regard the successful issue of evolution as completely predetermined in every detail. There is an option, and it is "the Great Option." The issue does depend partially on man's choice. The ascetic and mystical teaching of Teilhard is, then, entirely oriented to this choice: "to win the world of science for Christ," "to transfigure the agonizing immensity of the world into a center of loving energy," and "produce the organism of the total Christ." The wrong choice is described now as a "refusal of progression," and a withdrawal, a regression into "fusion" and inertia, cowardly annihilation of consciousness in pantheist mysticism, or else as a "Faustian individualism," a tenacious fixation on selfish interest, whether private or national, and a consequent refusal to "converge." But with his evolutionist perspective, Teilhard seems to take for granted that in the long run these refusals of individuals and groups will only contribute to the success of the whole process. The human race as such will, he feels, decide against entropy and enter into the superconscious life.

The great question is not whether this hope is laudable but whether it is purely and simply the theological hope of the Gospels and of the Church. With all his admiration for Teilhard, De Lubac does not go so far as to say that. He has many reservations about Teilhard's religious teaching style and its perspectives. But he accepts the Teilhardian wager as a *legitimate extrapolation* of Christian revelation in a modern context. Teilhard, in his estimation, has made an inspired guess and has built upon it a mystique of hope, which may well be of vital importance in our time. But De Lubac also admits that the enthusiasm of Teilhardians—and their overanxiety to be supermodern—has blinded them to two facts. Teilhard is not really as revolutionary as he himself thought, and one of the defects of Teilhardism is precisely its tendency to black-and-white schematization, a naïve polarization of "yesterday" and "tomorrow." The only harsh word De Lubac has for Teilhard is that he was too complacent about his own originality and that he neglected to learn from predecessors he would have agreed with, had he but known them: "His knowledge of Christian thought throughout the centuries was never more than elementary."

Rebirth and the New Man
in Christianity

One of the most important and characteristic themes of Christianity is that of the renewal of the self, the "new creation" of the Christian "in Christ." The all-too-familiar oversimplification of Christian belief, which makes it seem to be a formalistic method of gaining for oneself a place "in the other world" as a reward for good work and sufferings in the present life, obscures the real meaning of the Christian's metanoia, his participation in the death and resurrection of Christ by baptism and the eucharistic life of self-forgetfulness and fraternal love. This death to the "old self" and new life in the Spirit sent by Christ "from the Father" means not only a juridical salvation "in heaven" and "in the hereafter" but much more a new dimension of one's present life, a transformation and renewal not only of the Christian as a person but of the community of believers, the brotherhood of those who have received "the Spirit of Christ" and live in "the grace of Christ."

This renewal of life cannot be understood if it is seen merely as a ritual affair, the result of certain formal, exterior acts (though to some Christians it means little more than this). Nor is it an emotional conversion followed by adherence to a set of new attitudes and convictions, based on this sense of inner liberation (though here again some Christians attach undue importance to somewhat superficial psychological experiences and seek to bring them about).

In the theology of the New Testament, particularly that of Paul and John, the "new being" of the Christian, his "new creation," is the effect of an inner revolution which, in its ultimate and most radical significance, implies complete self-transcendence and transcendence of the norms and attitudes of any given culture, any merely human society. This includes transcendence even of religious practices. The whole sense of Paul's polemic with Judaism, a theology of grace which (through Augustine and Luther) has had a decisive effect in shaping Western culture, lies in his contention that the Christian who has attained a radical experience of liberty "in the Spirit" is no longer "under the law." He is henceforth superior to the laws and norms of any religious society, since he is bound by the higher law of love, which is his freedom itself, directed not merely to the fulfillment of his own will but rather to the transcendent and mysterious purposes of the Spirit: i.e., the good of all men. For all men are now seen as created, redeemed, and loved by God, and all are "one in Christ" in the sense that all are known to God as One Man, the universal Man, Christ, the Son of God. The theological implications of this are, of course, extremely subtle and complex. We cannot go into them here. The purpose of these few pages is merely to recall the special importance of this aspect of Christianity. The idea of "new birth" is at the very heart of Christianity, and has consequences of profound importance. If this is forgotten—as it so often is—then not only the individual Christian believer but also the Christian community and the society which has traditionally been regarded as Christian all become involved in inner contradictions which eventually lead to crisis. This, in turn, means that many will begin to experience their Christian life as an insoluble problem from which they either escape by disbelief or which they try to meet by some kind of emotionalism or doctrinaire rigidity.

Spiritual rebirth is the key to the aspirations of all the higher religions. By "higher religions" I mean those which, like Buddhism, Hinduism, Judaism, Islam, and Christianity, are not content with the ritual tribal cults rooted in the cycle of the seasons and harvests. These "higher religions" answer a deeper need in man: a need that cannot be satisfied merely by the ritual celebration of man's oneness with nature—his joy in the return of spring! Man seeks to be liberated from mere natural necessity, from servitude to fertility and seasons, from the round of birth, growth, and death. Man is not content with slavery to need: making his living, raising his family, and leaving a good name to his posterity. There is in the depths of man's heart a voice which says: "You must be born again." It is the obscure but insistent demand of his own nature to transcend itself in the freedom of a fully integrated, autonomous, personal identity.

When, in St. John's Gospel, Christ says to the Doctor of the Law Nicodemus: "You must be born again," He was not only telling him clearly something that he could hear, if he listened, in the silence and meditation of his own heart. He was also telling him that ordinary answers were not sufficient to meet his demand. To be "born again" is more than a matter of good moral resolutions, of self-discipline, of adjustment to social demands and requirements, of finding oneself a respected and worthwhile role in society. The summons to be "born again" does indeed make itself heard in our hearts, but it does not always have the same meaning, because we are not always capable of interpreting it in its true depth. Sometimes it is little more than an expression of weariness, a sense of failure, an awareness of wrong, a half-hopeless wish that one might get another chance, a fresh start. One desires to begin a new life because the burden of the old has now become an unbearable accumulation of fatigue, mistakes, betrayals, evasions, disappointments. One longs for a new life because the old life is stale, unworthy, uninteresting, cheap. One looks for a new way because all the old familiar ways are a dead end.

Unfortunately, this weariness with the old, this longing for the new, is often just another trap of nature, another variation in the imprisonment we would like to escape. It may inspire us with bright hopes, and it may induce us to believe we have found a new answer: but then, after a while, the same despair regains possession of our heart. Or else we simply fall back into the same old routine. Modern commercial society is built largely on the exploitation of this deep need for "new life" in the heart of man. But by exploiting this need, manipulating and intensifying it, the marketing society also aggravates and corrupts it at the same time. The need for "the new" becomes meretricious and false. It is at the same time insatiable and deceptive. It is tantalized and kept in a state of excitement by all kinds of clever techniques, and it never receives anything but pseudosatisfactions. Man has more and more needs, more and more hopes, and yet he has become more and more suspicious, less and less able to bear the burden of anxieties and half truths which he carries about in his heart. He feels himself a prisoner in himself, depressed and weighed down by the falsity and illusion of his own life. He knows he needs more desperately than ever to be "a new man" and yet he has lost all real hope of renewal. When he reaches out in desperation for something that promises to renew his jaded existence, he finds himself betrayed again. In the end, he takes to the easier forms of escape. He tries to evade the summons he still hears, however faintly, within his heart.

Man in modern technological society has begun to be callous and disillusioned. He has learned to suspect what claims to be new, to doubt all the "latest" in everything. He is drawn instinctively to the new, and yet he sees in it nothing but the same old sham. The specious glitter of newness, the pretended creativity of a society in which youthfulness is commercialized and the young are old before they are twenty, fills some hearts with utter despair. There seems to be no way to find any real change. "The more things change," says a French proverb, "the more they are the same."

Yet in the deepest ground of our being we still hear the insistent voice which tells us: "You must be born again."

There is in us an instinct for newness, for renewal, for a liberation of creative power. We seek to awaken in ourselves a force which really changes our lives from within. And yet the same instinct tells us that this change is a recovery of that which is deepest, most original, most personal in ourselves. To be born again is not to become somebody else, *but to become ourselves*.

The deepest spiritual instinct in man is that urge of inner truth which demands that he be faithful to himself: to his deepest and most original potentialities. Yet at the same time, in order to become oneself, one must die. That is to say, in order to become one's true self, the false self must die. In order for the inner self to appear, the outer self must disappear: or at least become secondary, unimportant.

How does one do this? In modern secular life, men resort to many expedients. If you have a great deal of money and can afford a long analysis—and can find an especially good psychoanalyst—it is possible that you may arrive at a psychological breakthrough and liberation, a recovery of authenticity and independence. But in reality, psychoanalysis and psychiatry are often content to compromise, happy if they can enable us to adjust without having to change or grow. We are not born again, we simply learn to put up with ourselves. Well, that is already something!

More usually the desperation of modern man drives him to seek a kind of new life and rebirth in mass movements, sometimes of an extremist character, sometimes messianic and political and quasi-religious. In these he tries to forget himself, in dedication to a more or less idealistic cause. But he is not born again, because true rebirth is a spiritual and religious transformation, far beyond the level of an ideology or a political "cause."

In the Gospel of St. John, we read the conversation in which Jesus speaks of man's new birth. It is a conversation with one of the leading scholars of the Jews, who came by night to speak with Jesus in secret. Nicodemus, the scholar, begins by saying that he recognizes Jesus as a true master sent by God. Jesus dismisses this as a statement of no importance. He does not seek the veneration of disciples. He says there is something of much more crucial importance than being the disciple of a spiritual master, however great. A man must be born again, or in a better translation, "born from above" (John 3:3).

Nicodemus, the scholar, asks in bewilderment: "How can a grown man be born? Can he go back into his mother's womb and be born again?" This is a natural question of a man who knows life in the world and is suspicious of spiritual and "mystical" delusions. We cannot reverse our course. We cannot really change (he thinks): all we can do is find some better ideal, some discipline, some new set of practices or ideas which will enable us to live the same life with less trouble and fewer mistakes.

But Jesus contradicts this in very forceful language:

Unless a man is born through water and the Spirit
He cannot enter the Kingdom of God.
What is born of flesh is flesh;

What is born of Spirit is spirit.
Do not be surprised when I say
You must be born from above.
The wind blows where ever it pleases;
You hear its sound
But you cannot tell where it comes from or where it is going.
That is how it is with all who are born of the Spirit. (JOHN 3:5–8)

In other words, what Jesus speaks of is an entirely new kind of birth. It is a birth which gives definitive meaning to life. The first birth, of the body, is a preparation for the second birth, the spiritual awakening of mind and heart. This is not to be confused with the awakening of rational consciousness which makes a human being responsible for his actions as an individual. It is a deep spiritual consciousness which takes man beyond the level of his individual ego. This deep consciousness, to which we are initiated by spiritual rebirth, is an awareness that we are not merely our everyday selves but we are also one with One who is beyond all human and individual self-limitation.

To be born again is to be born beyond egoism, beyond selfishness, beyond individuality, in Christ. To be born of flesh is to be born into the human race and to our society, with its fighting, its hatreds, its loves, its passions, its struggle, its appetites. To be born of the spirit is to be born into God (or the Kingdom of God) beyond hatred, beyond struggle, in peace, love, joy, self-effacement, service, gentleness, humility, strength.

How does this birth take place? By the water of baptism (which may well be a baptism solely of "desire," that is to say, a spiritual awakening in which the spirit is "washed" and renewed in God) and by the coming of the Spirit which is, in Jesus' words, as unpredictable and as unexpected as the wind. The Spirit moves constantly over the face of the whole earth, and though He makes use of human messengers, He is not bound to them or limited to them. He can act without them.

At this point we must observe that the rebirth of which Christ speaks is not a single event but a continuous dynamic of inner renewal. Certainly, sacramental baptism, the "birth by water," can be given only once. But birth in the Spirit happens many times in a man's life, as he passes through successive stages of spiritual development. A false and superficial view of Christianity assumes that it is enough to be baptized with water and to observe certain ethical and ritual prescriptions in order to guarantee for oneself a happy life in the other world. But this is only a naïve view of Christianity. True Christianity is growth in the life of the Spirit, a deepening of the new life, a continuous rebirth, in which the exterior and superficial life of the ego-self is discarded like an old snake skin and the mysterious, invisible self of the Spirit becomes more present and more active. The true Christian rebirth is a renewed transformation, a "passover" in which man is progressively liberated from selfishness and not only grows in love but in some sense "becomes love." The perfection of the new birth is reached where there is no more selfishness, there is only love. In the language of the mystics, there is no more ego-self, there is only Christ; self no longer acts, only the Spirit acts in pure love. The perfect illumination is, then, the illumination of Love shining by itself. To become completely transparent and allow Love to shine by itself is the maturity of the "New Man."

Nicodemus, the scholar, could not understand. He had an active, ego-centered view of perfection. His life was based on the observance of strict religious law, and the understanding of this law depended on correct interpretation. Thus, there was need for many experts and trained legal minds to help everyone keep the law in its every detail. Jesus was speaking of something quite different: of a Spirit who came like the wind, invisible, unpredictable, and who transformed one's whole life.

"You must be born of the Spirit."

It is not enough to remain the same "self," the same individual ego, with a new set of activities and a new lot of religious practices. One must be born of the Spirit, who is free, and who reaches the inmost depths of the heart by taking that heart to Himself, by making Himself one with our heart, by creating for us, invisibly, a new identity: by being Himself that identity (1 Corinthians 2:6–16; 2 Corinthians 3:12–18; Romans 8:14–17, etc.).

Nicodemus thought this was impossible. Jesus then rebuked him, because he claimed to be a scholar and an expert in those truths which explain the meaning of man's existence and yet he did not know this elementary truth of religious existence. The life of man has no meaning if he is simply born in the flesh, born into the human race, without being born of the Spirit, or born into God.

The famous Japanese Zen scholar, Daisetz Suzuki, had a deep appreciation of this idea of the "birth of God" in man, as expressed by the Rhenish mystics. In this, Dr. Suzuki was much less like Nicodemus than many Christian scholars: he penetrated one essential aspect of Christianity and saw its true meaning. His Zen doubtless gave him this understanding. This is perhaps also true of Kitaro Nishida, one of the great Japanese philosophers of our century, who likewise saw the deeper dimensions of Christianity.

But the argument between Christ and Nicodemus is renewed in every century. Each age has the answer to Nicodemus: "How can a man be born again? How can he enter again into his mother's womb?" In other words, every age has official ideological answers that seek to evade the necessity of the divine birth. The human birth is enough: then one needs only to seek a political, or ethical, or doctrinal, or philosophical answer. Or one needs only to seek a new drug, a new pleasure, a new love affair, a new experience. Even Christians themselves have at times followed Nicodemus rather than Christ, when they identified Christianity with a given social or political or economic structure, or with a mere ideological system. But whenever a certain group of Christians has done this, then other men, strangers and new converts, have come to answer to the call of the Spirit. These others have been more attentive to the quiet secret voice speaking softly as the wind. They have been willing to risk everything in order to be born again, not in the flesh, but in God.

The Christian civilization of the West has incorporated into itself a great deal of the spiritual dynamism of the Christian faith. "New life" has been interpreted as "new activity" and a more fruitful productive existence. If the tree is known by its fruits, then surely a new life, a new being, must manifest itself in a new kind of fruitfulness. The Christian metanoia must liberate unsuspected spiritual energies. It would be tempting to explore the way in which the prophetic, charismatic fruitfulness which were the signs of "the Spirit" in early, eschatological Christianity, have been transformed and secularized—even institutionalized—throughout the centuries of development of Christian culture. The prophetic and other charisms of the early Church—signs of freedom from the domination of Roman and Hellenic culture—gradually merged with the cultural energies first of Rome, then of the northern barbarians. In the fateful clash with Islam, Germanic Christianity became a crusading religion. Renaissance Christendom set out to conquer the world and subject it to the Cross. The charismata of the early Church had turned into the pseudocharism of conquest and of success. Thus, Christian culture itself has been increasingly dynamic and activistic, and "rebirth"—which remains a central fact of Christian existence—tends to be interpreted in aggressive, activistic, rather than passive, contemplative terms.

The West has lived for thousands of years under the sign of the Titan, Prometheus, the fire stealer, the man of power who defies heaven in order to get what he himself desires. The West has lived under the sign of will, the love of power, action, and domination. Hence, Western Christianity has often been associated with a spiritual will-to-power and an instinct for organization and authority. This has taken good forms, in devotion to works of education, healing the sick, building schools, order and organization in religion itself. But even the good side of activism has tended toward an over-emphasis on will, on action, on conquest, on "getting things done," and this in turn has resulted in a sort of religious restlessness, pragmatism, and the worship of visible results.

There is another essential aspect of Christianity: the interior, the silent, the contemplative, in which hidden wisdom is more important than practical organizational science, and in which love replaces the will to get visible results. The New Man must not be a one-sided and aggressive activist: he must also have depth, he must be able to be silent, to listen to the secret voice of the Spirit. He must renounce his own will to dominate and let the Spirit act secretly in and through him. This aspect of Christianity will perhaps be intelligible to those in an Asian culture who are familiar with the deeper aspects of their own religious tradition. Hence, the crucial importance of a Christian dialogue in depth with Asian religion. For the religions of Asia also have long sought to liberate man from imprisonment in a half-real external existence in order to initiate him into the full and complete reality of an inner peace which is secret and beyond explanation.

The Climate of Mercy

FOR ALBERT SCHWEITZER

The mercy of God in Christ is more than forensic absolution from sin. To be called to become a new man and to participate in a new creation is, precisely, the work of mercy and not of power. Mercy is, then, not only forgiveness, but life. It is more than that. It is the epiphany of hidden truth and of God's redeeming Love for man. It is the revelation of God Himself, not as an infinite nature, as a "Supreme Being," and as ultimate, absolute power, but as Love, as Creator and Father, as Son and Savior, as Life-giving Spirit. Mercy is, then, not simply something we deduce from a previously apprehended concept of the divine Essence ("If he is the Supreme Being, then it follows that he is supremely loving, etc. . . ."), but an event in which God reveals himself to us in His redemptive love and in the great gift which is the outcome of this event: our mercy to others. Indeed, there is but one center of all mercy, one merciful event, in which we receive mercy and give it, or give it and receive it (Matthew 5:7; 6:12–14; 18:21–35). This event is the saving mystery of the Cross, which alone enables us to enter into a true spiritual harmony with one another, seeing one another not only in natural fellowship but in the Spirit and mercy of Christ, who emptied Himself for us and became obedient even to death (Philippians 2:2–8). The patristic theology of

grace, expressed in terms of the restoration of the divine likeness to man created in the image of God and defaced by sin,
must be seen in the light of this Christ-like mercy. We are
"perfect as our heavenly Father is perfect," in proportion as
our love is no longer restricted by a "law" or a "measure"
of recognizable self-interest. If we love others only insofar as
they love us, we are confined within an iron law of selfhood
which seeks to assert our own existence and defend it (however hopelessly) against extinction. The love we thus give to
others is the reward we offer them, the payment with which
we buy their recognition of our own existence. With such
love we only bribe them to help us persist in an illusion of a
deathless and complete autonomy. And we bribe them by
helping them defend the same illusion in themselves. But the
Father makes His sun rise on the evil and the good, and our
love, if we are to be sons of God, must not be limited to
friends and to those who favor us or give us joy. Christian
mercy falls like rain on the just and the unjust and has no
law but sonship, likeness to the "perfect" Father (Matthew
5:43–48). Mercy, in other words, is at work in the freedom
of the sons of God, is the full expression of that freedom, its
character, its proper name, the reflection of the truth that
makes us free (the truth of the merciful God revealing Himself in the eschatological event which is mercy and salvation).

To receive mercy and to give it is, then, to participate, as
son of the Father, in the work of the new creation and of
redemption. It is to share in the eschatological fulfillment
of the work of Christ and in the establishment of the Kingdom. But without mercy, on the other hand, no zeal, no
doctrine, no work, no sacrifice has in it the savor of life. It
tastes of death, of *vetustas,* of the old things that have been
done away with in the victory of the Risen Christ. No structure can stand that is not built on the rock of God's mercy
and steadfast love (*hesed*), and his unfailing promises.

Some English mystic of the fourteenth century has described the mercy of God in these words: "He abideth patiently, he forgiveth easily, he understandeth mercifully, he forgeteth utterly." In these simple and profound words, mercy is identified with God's knowledge of the sinner. It is not only that God looking down on the sinner as a wretched object decrees forgiveness but that He *understands mercifully*. His mercy is not merely an annulment of unpleasant facts, a refusal to see an evil that is really there. It is more: it is a seeing of the inner meaning of evil not as an entity in itself but as an incident in a saving event, as the *felix culpa* of the paschal "Exsultet." Sin is not, then, a powerful and autonomous adversary of God's mercy, one against which mercy might conceivably find itself helpless, one against which power and justice, the panoply of might and hate, ought perhaps ultimately to be displayed. God does not gaze with grim and implacable revulsion into the heart of the sinner to discern there the "thing" or the "being" which He hates. He understands the sinner mercifully, that is to say, that His look penetrates the whole being of the sinner with mercy from within so that the inmost reality of the sinner is no longer sinfulness but sonship. Then the power of mercy is free to draw the sinful existent into identity with his inmost being. Alienation is overcome. The sinful consciousness becomes capable of seeing itself face to face with the truth, without fear and without hate, because without division. The mercy of God shows the sinner to himself, no longer as existentially opposed to truth but as reconcilable with it. He becomes able to see himself as having an inner being in which truth is present. He recognizes himself as capable of a grace-filled existence, blessed by mercy, in which outward action is reconciled with inmost being. He ceases to look upon himself, whether rightly or wrongly, as a self-contradictory thing, and indeed he is absolved from the contradiction already implied by the tendency to scrutinize himself as object. This reconciliation is the ontological heart of mercy. When the sinful *Dasein* is aware of itself as understood mercifully and as "seen" full of mercy by its Creator and Redeemer, then the evil of sin, the curse of death, are "forgotten utterly." But no man can cure his own heart and deliver his own conscience from the incubus of evil merely by self-analysis and by catharsis, or merely by opening his heart to the understanding of a brother. The mercy of God must wipe out the writing that is graven in his own consciousness, and deep beneath it in the unconscious depths of his very existence. Mercy is the word of life that not only annuls the verdict of guilt but the sentence of death printed in our existence. Not that we do not die: but death itself becomes the crowning event of a saved life and the door to spirit, being, and truth in the Cross of Christ (Philippians 3:7–12).

Yet we are sinners, and we are always menaced by the dreadful power of sin, which but for God's mercy would resume its tyrannical reign in our hearts.

The alienated human existent (not fully alive to himself as being and therefore not capable of full and personal realization) requires mercy in order to get beyond the mere habit of vegetative existence. Man finds himself in the transit, the *pascha,* or passover from habitual and routine acceptance, the free and spiritual affirmation of himself as a being grounded in mercy and therefore endowed with a plenary meaning. This plenary meaning, however, takes the individual out of himself as a datum engaged in a futile struggle to endow itself with significance and plunges him into the significance with which love and mercy have saturated and irradiated man's collective being through the Resurrection of Christ.

The human existent is redeemed and delivered into the full freedom of the Christian person when it is liberated from the demonic and futile project of self-redemption—the self-contradictory and self-defeating enterprise of establishing itself in unassailable security as if its existence were identical with being, and as if it were completely autonomous. This hateful enterprise is carried on by the existent maintaining itself as "being" and as autonomous self-fulfillment, challenging and defying every other existent, seeking either to dominate or to placate all that it confronts. This implies a constant wearying effort at deception, with eager thrusts of passion and power, constantly frustrated and falling back into the cunning futility of trying to outwit reality itself.

Legal virtuousness is one of the ways in which the human existent seeks to carry out this project of deception and to gain mastery over the death that is inexorably present in the very fact of bodily life itself. There are other, more complex spiritual ways of attempting this same deception: subtle ascetic techniques, Tantric, magic, theosophical, gnostic disciplines: they are numberless, the ways in which man seeks to escape the inexorable condemnation. All are self-defeating except the Gospel mercy, in which the self-seeking self is liberated from its search and its concern, therefore to some extent from anguish, by *finding* not self but truth in Christ. This "finding" is the discovery, in grace and faith, that one is "mercifully understood" and that in the Spirit of this mercy and this understanding one is enabled to understand others in mercy and in pity. The weakness and defenselessness in our hearts, which make us pitiless to others, are then dispelled not by power but by trust in the divine mercy, which is given us when we no longer seek to defend our defenselessness, and are ready to accept our own boundless need in a merciful exchange with others whose poverty is as great as our own!

Man is fallen into self-contradiction and ambiguity from which no self-study, no individualistic or social ethic, no philosophy, no mere mysticism can liberate him. His Christian calling is not a calling to self-purification or to good works,

to the elimination of sensual desires, to the cleansing of concepts, to the emptying of the intellect and will, to ultimate
inner tranquillity, and to liberation from slavery to cravings.
On the contrary, his very tendency to understand the meaning of liberation in such terms may ultimately make liberation impossible.

This is a view of life, essentially "under sin," because it is
under the old Law, by which Law gives sin and passion the
appearance of liberty. For whenever the Law says, "Thou
shalt not," there springs up in the heart of self-alienated man
a doubt, and an occasion, a project of self-recovery and self-
fulfillment of defiance of the Law. The promises, menaces,
and demands of the Law are ambiguous because they point
to self-possession and suggest two conflicting possible ways
to autonomy: one by following the Law and the other by
defying it. It is always possible for man under the Law, in
his fallenness and confusion, to outline projects of liberty
"against" the Law. But these are illusory projects which receive their apparent substance from the Law in its promises
or in its threats. Thus, the Law tends to become an incite-
ment to a despairing self-realization. It incites the self-seeking
self to plunge into its own void. The very Law itself per-
versely and cruelly seems to define this void as "liberty" and
"realization," for it tells man that he can "choose" sin and
that, therefore, sinning is a form of freedom. Why this illusion? Because at the same time the Law offers a deceptive
promise of fulfillment to the self-seeking self in legal righteousness. The Law is a guarantee of respectability, security,
and power, and to keep the Law is to enter into the human
and social structure which is founded on the Law and provides its rewards and sanctions. It is to share the power that
belongs to the "elements of the world" (forgetting that they
are at best "feeble elements") or even worse, perhaps, the
power of the *archontes* (Ephesians 1:21). The Law offers the

self-seeking self the spurious autonomy which comes from creating a place for itself in the minds of men by human righteousness and achievements: he who is justified by the Law is understood not mercifully but righteously, not by God, but by men (God says "I know you not"). He receives his reward (Matthew 6:16). This reward may be a righteous unbelief, the hardening of the heart in self-respect ("How can you believe who seek glory one from another?"). At the same time, this hardening issues in a deceptive dialogue of claims and demands with others who tend to accept this self-righteousness at its own evaluation. They accept the Law or rebel against it as it appears, incarnate in those who claim they have been justified by it.

Thus, Law without mercy kills mercy in the hearts of those who seek justification solely by socially acceptable virtuousness and by courting the favor of authority. This legal holiness, in its turn, destroys the hope of mercy in those who despair of the Law.

We must, therefore, remember the religious and Christian importance of not implicitly identifying external "Law" with interior "Mercy," either in our doctrine (and in this we usually manage to keep them distinct) or in our lives (here we tend in practice to confuse them by making the fulfillment of the Law's inexorable demand either a condition for receiving mercy or a guarantee that one has received it).

In actual fact, as St. Thomas points out, mercy and grace *are* the New Law—a perfect Law—binding on the Christian insofar as the other laws, in all that they have of life and meaning, are fulfilled in mercy and love. The Old Law, says St. Thomas, gave the *precept* of charity and mercy, but the New Law is the spring of the Holy Spirit Himself to dwell in our hearts, fulfilling Himself the command to love by giving us the power to do what was otherwise impossible (I–II, 107, 1, ad 2). "What are the (new) laws of God written in the hearts of men," Augustine asks, "if not the very presence of the Holy Spirit?" (*De Spiritu et Libera,* 21). Hence, the Law of Mercy is not an extrinsically given imperative but an inner power, not an inexorable demand imposed on a weak and confused nature but a personal inclination to love imparted by the presence of the Spirit of Sonship who makes us free, liberating us from the tyranny of natural weakness and of existential demands for self-assertion (Romans 8:2ff).

The whole climate of the New Testament is one of liberation by mercy: liberation, through God's grace and free gift, from sin, death, and even from the Old Law. The miraculous acts of Christ in the synoptics tend generally to make this clear. The power of forgiveness is clearly associated with the power of healing and restoring to life (Mark 2:5–12). The climate of the Gospel is, then, a climate at once of mercy and of life, of forgiveness and creativity. We enter into this climate and breathe its pure air by faith, which is submission to the "New Law" of grace and forgiveness, that is to say, submission to a Law of accepting and being accepted, loving and being loved, in a personal encounter with the Lord of Life and with our brother in him. This is a "Law" in a broad and analogical sense, because it is governed not so much by fixed and abstract patterns as by the existential demands of personal love and loyalty: demands of grace and of the heart which are defined to a great extent by our own history of personal sin, need, and forgiveness. To relinquish the personal fidelity owed to Christ's grace to us in our own life, in order to return to an impersonal and abstract forensic standard, is to renounce freedom and fall back into servility and so to annul the gift of God, at the same time declaring by implication that the Cross of Christ was meaningless (Galatians 2:21). To refuse mercy is to fail in faith.

The Church, which Christ has "purchased with his blood"

(Acts 2:29), is called to keep alive on earth this irreplaceable climate of mercy, truth, and faith in which the creative and life-giving joy of reconciliation in Christ always not only remains possible but is a continuous and ever-renewed actuality. This power of mercy, reconciliation, and oneness in Christ is identified with the power which raised the Lord Himself from the dead (Ephesians 1:19–20; 2:2), and vanquished the "power" of the *archontes,* the tyrannical spirits who rule "this world of darkness" and dominate over the sons of unbelief and disobedience (Ephesians 2:2). The power of mercy is the power that makes us one in Christ, destroying all divisions (Ephesians 2:14–18). Christ in His death on the Cross put an end in His own body to the conflict generated by the Law and its observances. Our access to Him is by the way of acceptance, through the mystery of the Cross (Philippians 3:9–10; Ephesians 2:16). When we enter the "fellowship of His sufferings" we receive power from God to "live together with Christ . . . in the heavenly sphere," which is the fruit of His great love, "rich in mercy" (Ephesians 2:4ff).

But if we have received mercy, and have entered into the life of the Church in order at once to share and to proclaim the riches of mercy which make the Church the pleroma of Christ (Ephesians 1:9–12), then we must show by our mercy to others that we realize what the Christ life really means. We show that we live in the climate of creative love, the climate of the Church, to the extent that we experience the truth that it is "more blessed to give than to receive" (Acts 20:35).

Fr. M. A. Couturier (the Dominican apostle of sacred art, not the ecumenist) declared with perfect truth that many Christians "are enclosed in their Church and in their faith as others are enclosed in their Party. They aspire to a totalitarian state: and none of this has anything to do with the Gospel." In fact, the climate of totalism, which as we know to our own cost can very easily become that of religion itself, is a climate of security purchased by servile resignation under human power: obedience to the authority of might rather than freedom in the climate of life-giving love and mercy. This, of course, raises a most difficult, not to say most urgent, problem of authority in the visible structure of the Church. There must obviously be some visible authority and there must be some form of law in any institutional structure. This authority and law must be justified, as also the sacraments and the sabbath are, by being *propter homines*. They must serve only to protect and preserve the climate of mercy, or life-giving forgiveness and reconciliation. Hence, authority and power become abusive when they become ends in themselves to which the good of persons becomes subservient: when, in other words, souls for whom Christ died are allowed to be destroyed in order that power may be preserved intact.

The climate of mercy, which is the climate of the new creation, depends on the realization that *all men are acceptable before God,* since the Word was made man, dwelt among us, died on the Cross for us, rose from the dead, and is enthroned in our flesh, our humanity, in the glory of God. Hence, all that is required for a man to be acceptable before God, and a recipient of mercy, is for him to be a man and a sinner. (I did not come to call the just, but sinners . . . Matthew 9:13; Romans 5:8). We ourselves are not entitled to be more demanding than God. Whoever is acceptable to Him is, therefore, acceptable to us, and this is the test of our faith and of our obedience to Him (John 15:12, 17; 12:34–35), that we become to some extent able to be merciful to others as He has been merciful to us, knowing that this mercy is the cohesive power that establishes and manifests the Father's love in the living and unified Mystical Body of the Son (John 17:11–12, 21–22).

Hence, if a man is to be acceptable to us, nothing more is required than that he need our mercy, whether he himself is aware of this or not. It is not required that he be a certain type of man, belonging to a special race, or class, even religious customs (Galatians 5:6). Least of all is it required that he be exactly like ourselves, friendly toward us, and disposed to flatter us with a privileged consideration of our person and our ideas. The implicit demand which we formulate by asserting our own justice, setting ourselves up as a law by which to judge and evaluate other men, kills mercy in our hearts and in theirs. If I set myself up inexorably as a law to my brother, then I cannot help trying to interfere with his life by occult violence, malice, and deceit. I set myself up as a potential *power* to which I demand some form, be it only symbolic, of homage and submission. I set myself up, in particular, as a virtuous example which defines and identifies my brother's sin—for that in which he differs from me becomes at once "sin." Note what I do in this: I arrogate to myself a right to *make him a sinner*. I take to myself the awful power which Paul ascribed to the law, of *bringing to life sin in my fellow man* (Romans 7:8–10). Nor is this power illusory. It is most real and most malevolent in strong collective groups whose ideologies can create a bad conscience and even a sense of guilt and self-hate in supposedly "lesser breeds without the law." We have seen this force at work in colonialism and in racism, where the arrogance of unscrupulous and self-righteous power has deeply wounded the consciousness of millions of men. From these deep wounds will spring new "laws" of violence, hatred, and revenge.

In the climate which is not that of life and mercy, but of death and condemnation, the personal and collective guilts of men and of groups wrestle with one another in death struggle. Men, tribes, nations, sects, parties set themselves up in forms of existence which are mutual accusations. They thus seek survival and self-affirmation by living demonically, for the demon is the "accuser of the brethren." A demonic existence is one which insistently diagnoses what it cannot cure, what it has no desire to cure, what it seeks only to bring to full potency in order that it may cause the death of its victim. Yet this is the temptation which besets the sin-ridden *Dasein* of man, for whom a resentful existence implies the need and the decision to accuse and to condemn all other existences. Note here the peril of the tyrannical concept of God as a mere limited "existent" among other existents. Such a God becomes a tribal totem, a magnification of the self-seeking existent striving to establish its autonomy in its own void. Can such a God be anything but the embodiment of resentments, hatreds, and dreads? It is in the presence of such idols that vindictive and death-dealing orthodoxies flourish. These gods of party and sect, race and nation, are necessarily the gods of war.

There is a false and demonic mercy, then, which grows in the soil of this kind of accusing existence, an existence forfeit to self-complacency and contempt, an existence rooted in resentment, hatred, and war. Such mercy, having (let us suppose) successfully awakened guilt in the other, absolves the guilt when sufficient gestures of submission have been extorted from him by force or manipulation. But it is not Christian mercy to create a bad conscience in my brother and then entice him by pardon into my own poisoned bosom, admitting him into the stifling climate of my own lovelessness.

This demonic falsification of mercy constitutes one of the most serious religious problems of our era. Indeed, the whole future of the Christian missionary apostolate is hanging on the solution of the ambiguities that have arisen from this. The solution cannot even be guessed at until the problem itself is faced, and the times are forcing us to face it. It is the problem of the inevitable and often perfectly sincere confusion that once identified the Gospel with Christian and Western cultural values. The bitter truth of Auschwitz and Hiroshima has begun, it seems, to clarify this situation. Even to the blindest among us, the confusion is beginning to be evident.

One fruit of this evidence is that the mercy which we often think we are bringing to men is less merciful than we believed, and that it is we, in fact, who most need to receive mercy from those to whom we have preached it. The grace of the word preached to Africa is perhaps the paradoxical realization of our own sin, our own need to be pardoned, and in particular our immense need to be pardoned by Africa.

Made in the context of an essay honoring Albert Schweitzer, such a statement might seem to be either unnecessarily romantic or simply out of place. At any rate, he better than any other would be able to say if there is truth in it. The grace of his particular vocation is a grace of solitude and uniqueness. Neither solitude nor uniqueness is ever comfortable: there is always the risk that such isolation might be prophetic, fraught with prophetic silence and doubts, moments of self-questioning abandonment and of dread. One's very isolation may seem an accusation of others who are "not there" and others in turn who are not there may take occasion, from the unique case of a Schweitzer, to justify their absence and their inertia. On the shoulder of this one man, and of perhaps a handful of others like him, has fallen the whole burden of white Christendom. Such a burden is not only a responsibility but even a temptation, a temptation which the rest of us must thank him for facing. His vocation (a monk may be permitted to say this) is in the most authentic monastic tradition of *peregrinatio,* exile, solitude, and love. We must not forget that works of mercy were combined with solitude not only in the ideal of Basilian monachism but in that of Syria, Egypt, and of the Benedictine West. It is such uncompromising sacrifice and renunciation that confer upon the monk the right to perform good works that have a monastic and charismatic dimension, not reducible to the mere official ministrations of the paid functionary, however dedicated he may be.

At no time can the mystery of mercy be understood if we become obsessed with finding out who is the creditor and who is the debtor. The climate of mercy becomes life-giving and creative when men realize that they are all debtors, and that the debt is unpayable. (St. Anselm, who is too often accused of having fabricated a completely legalistic soteriology, was actually making this point clear.) Only in the Cross are all debts paid, and there are no solutions between man and man, or man and God, that can fully satisfy the claims of mercy and redemptive, reconciling love as if they were the demands of commutative justice. The claims of mercy are demands in a totally new sense: demands not that the debt be properly measured and then generously paid, but that *the whole root of indebtedness* be laid open to the light that "understandeth mercifully" and thus seen to be quite other than we thought. There can be no question of a limit to pardon—a pardon that becomes meaningless and ineffectual after "seven times" (Matthew 18:21). We seek that divine mercy which, enduring forever (Psalms 106:1), and dynamically active as a leaven in history, has entirely changed the aspect of human existence, delivering it from its forfeiture to a syndrome of accusation, projection, resentment, and ultimate despair. We seek it not only in our hearts and minds but in man's world, his common life on earth.

Mercy heals in every way. It heals bodies, spirits, society, and history. It is the only force that can truly heal and save. It is the force that has been brought into the world in the great eschatological event of the Cross, in order that man might be totally renewed, and that the guilt-ridden and despairing *Dasein* of the lost human person might find itself reconciled in freedom and mercy with the needs and destinies of others and of the world itself. Mercy heals the root of life by curing our existence of the self-devouring despair which projects its own evil upon the other as a demand and an accusation.

When we are enabled by God's gift to become merciful, we are given the power to understand mercifully, to accept and to pardon the evil in others, not as a fruit of some godlike magnanimity rooted in our own justice, but first of all as the fruit of a self-knowledge which is liberated from the need to project its own evil upon the other.

After this, when we have learned not to see an evil which is perhaps not there in any case, we become able to see the same evil in ourselves, to accept it, to repent of it, and (knowing that we are understood mercifully) to forget utterly. The work of mercy is this understanding and this forgetfulness.

"The characters which accompany wealth," said Aristotle, "are plain for all to see. The wealthy are insolent and arrogant, being mentally affected by the acquisition of wealth, for they seem to think that they possess all good things; for wealth is a kind of standard of value of everything else so that everything seems purchasable by it." This is true not merely of individuals but of societies as well. The true "Law" of our day is the law of wealth and material power. The fate of men, indeed of mankind itself, depends on the laws of economics. It is the market that in reality determines the existence, indeed the survival, of all men and dictates the ideals and the actualities of social life. In our time the struggle of mercy is, then, not against rigid and inflexible morality but against a different and more subtle hardening of heart, a general loss of trust and of love that is rooted in greed and belief in money. What irony that this faith in money, this trust in the laws of the market, this love of wealth and power, should have come to be identified with Christianity and freedom in so many minds, as if the freedom to make money were the freedom of the sons of God, and as if (Bloy pointed this out) money had demonically usurped the role in modern society which the Holy Spirit is supposed to have in the Church.

The love of power and gain becomes the demonic pseudo-pneuma which leads men and institutions, ostensibly "Christian," to trample on the hearts of their fellow men, to destroy primitive social structures which had a semblance of equity, beauty, and order, leaving in their place nothing but slums built out of gasoline cans and ultimate degradation. Obedience to this "spirit" and to the social values which it inspires, whether in marketing nations or in totalistic societies, is servitude to an inhuman banality that is blind to the most elementary human instincts and insensitive to the most fundamental contacts (the infinitely banal "sanity" of an Eichmann, and the hideous caricature which was his "obedience"!). Our whole future, the very survival of humanity, appears mortgaged and *closed* by this demonic legalism, this blasphemous caricature of "order."

Can the power of evangelical mercy possibly break through this iron ring of satanic determinism? We must believe that it can, or else we are not fully Christians. But our optimism must not be utopian and sentimental. Obviously a mercy that is confined to the dimensions of individual piety can at best illuminate our abdication with a warm, sentimental glow. Today it is not enough for a few individuals to be kind, to understand, and to pardon. This can too easily become a sheer mystification, particularly if it seems to absolve everyone else from serious responsibility in social life.

Though there is no use placing our hopes on a totally utopian new world in which everyone is sublimely merciful, we are obliged as Christians to seek some way of giving the mercy and the compassion of Christ a social, even a political, dimension. The eschatological function of mercy, we repeat, is to prepare the Christian transformation of the world, and to usher in the Kingdom of God. This Kingdom is manifestly "not of this world" (all forms of millennial and messianic Christian optimism to the contrary), but it demands to be typified and prepared by such forms of heroic social witness that make Christian mercy plain and evident in the world.

But in a world of huge atomic stockpiles, a Christian mercy that confines itself to interior feelings of benevolence and "good intentions" in the use of appalling destructive power can manifestly not meet the demands of eschatological love. The only event that can be ushered in by this kind of sentimentality is too grim to be contemplated, and it belongs more to Antichrist than to the Kingdom of the risen Kyrios.

Christian mercy must discover, in faith, in the Spirit, a power strong enough to initiate the transformation of the world into a realm of understanding, unity, and relative peace, where men, nations, and societies are willing to make the enormous sacrifices required if they are to communicate intelligibly with one another, understand one another, cooperate with one another in feeding the hungry millions and in building a world of peace.

Such is the eschatological climate of the new creation, in which pardon replaces sacrifice (Osee 6:6; Matthew 9:13) and the whole world is filled with the mercy of God as the waters cover the sea.

The Good News of the Nativity

How is the Christian of the twentieth century to read the Gospels, and especially the Gospel story of the Nativity of Christ our Lord? This is not simply a trite question which an author may proceed to dismiss airily with a few familiar and optimistic generalities. It is a matter which seriously concerns every believer, since almost every Christian is now somehow aware that the Gospels, and the Nativity Gospels in particular, have been called into question as "myths." If that is the case, how are we to read them? Must we carefully consider each detail, examine what the critics have said, reject all they have rejected, keep only what they have all kept? We will thus conform ourselves to a decision of "science." But these critical certitudes will limit us to a low-protein diet of one or two authenticated facts upon which everybody *must* agree.

Is the modern Christian to sustain his faith on such Spartan nourishment? Or should he simply ignore all this, adopt a fundamentalist position, maintain that every word is to be taken literally, and perhaps even offer high-powered apologetic justifications for all those points which simple faith formerly accepted without question? This, unfortunately, is a rigid and artificial attitude which, while it may seem to recommend itself by its simplicity, lends itself to a distortion of the Christian message and ultimately lacks humility and respect for difficult realities.

It is doubtless rash for one who is not himself a Scripture scholar to raise such intricate questions when he cannot even begin to treat them technically. But the point is that, while there is every reason for a modern, critical, and technical approach to the Gospel text and literary forms, and while we must be grateful for the contribution of such scientific study, there remains for everyone, scholar or not, one way above all to read—or to *hear*—the Gospel of the Nativity: the way in which the Church has always read and heard it, in the celebration of the Christmas feast.

The Church did not in the beginning regard the Gospel narratives as strict scientific history but as kerygmatic recitals embodying the inerrant truth of revelation. She did not question the facts or the sincerity of those who narrated them—it was her own sincerity! She did not self-consciously reflect upon the narratives to determine how far they were historic and how far poetic. She was concerned with one truth—the revelation of God's saving love for man. The revelation of this truth was bound up with the related experience of those who had witnessed the events or had participated in the first fruits of the Spirit given to the faithful community. The Gospel of the Nativity, proclaimed today in the faithful assembly, makes present once again the Church's consciousness of her salvation in, and her oneness with, the incarnate Word. It is her confession and celebration of this great fact.

Let us say at once that we need not fear the demythologizers when it comes to understanding the Gospels in this sense. We will find, indeed, that their efforts, however radical they may seem and however we may disagree with them on certain points, have tended in general to bring out precisely this: the Gospel message is theologically relevant and its content is apprehended in a valid and truly evangelical manner when it is accepted by the believer in the way in which it was announced and declared by the Church in the beginning. However, the task of demythologizing appears to be a kind of semantic purification of this recital.

Since it is the office of the monk in the Church to keep alive this primitive awareness of the Bible, the experience of reading the Bible in *lectio divina* and "hearing" it in the celebration of the liturgy, we may confidently treat our subject as a "monastic reading" of the Nativity Gospels, not without giving modern criticism the attention due to it. This might seem to be, at first sight, a singularly difficult task. Were not the monks the worst of all offenders when it came to adding allegory to myth?

There is more than one kind of "monastic reading" of the Bible. Usually we think of the "monastic" or "contemplative" approach in terms of the Origenist tradition, which remained by far the most influential in the Middle Ages, which has been treated so thoroughly by Fr. De Lubac, and which is quite out of favor today. This is the typological, sometimes called "mystical" (and sometimes abusively "allegorical"), interpretation of the Scriptures. That will not be our direct concern here. There is another, simpler approach, that of the earlier monks (not all of whom were Origenists by any means), who simply wanted to hear the plain message of the Gospel, God's word in his Church, as announced in the Church and understood by the Church. They wanted to discover God as he revealed himself in his word, and not merely religious ideas about life and virtue ingeniously spun out of the sacred narrative.

From the beginning, the Church, and the monks with her, has regarded Biblical theology as a theology of kerygma, recital, and celebration. The theological content of the Bible is clarified above all by the ecclesiastical consciousness of the faithful, of the Church herself as the Bride of the Spirit, when "in the Spirit" the words inspired by the Spirit are understood and received in the hearts of all who participate in the liturgy. The homilies and expositions of the Fathers are to be read in this context. It is, indeed, in this atmosphere of proclamation and liturgy that the sacred texts themselves took shape. This is a fact which has been brought out precisely by form criticism.

The Gospel of the Nativity is, therefore, not merely the gentle, comforting story of a Virgin Mother and a sweet Babe lying in the manger, a story which appeals to our hearts and brings us back once a year to the simplicity of our own lost childhood. It is a solemn proclamation of an event which is the turning point of all history: the coming of the Messiah, the Anointed King and Son of God, the Word-made-Flesh, pitching his tent among us, not merely to seek and save that which was lost, but to establish his Kingdom, the eschatological Kingdom, the manifestation of the fullness of time and the completion of history. It is the announcement of a decisive eschatological event, a liberation from all incomplete and fragmentary religious forms, a deliverance from what Paul called mere "elements" of worldly religion and philosophy. With the coming of the Son of Man, the Church announces the completion of God's plan:

When the fullness of time came, God sent his Son, born of a woman, born subject to the Law, in order to redeem all those who were subject to the Law and to confer upon us the adoption of sons [GALATIANS 4:4–5].

The birth of the Son of God is, then, as the monastic writers of the Middle Ages well understood, following the Fathers of the Church, our own birth to a new status, an elevation of man to divine sonship, an opening out of entirely new possibilities for humanity in Christ, God, and Man.

The Nativity message is the message not only of joy but of *the* joy: the GREAT JOY which all the people of the world have always expected without fully realizing what it was. It is the joy of eschatological fulfillment which we seek, in the depths of our hearts, from the moment that we are beings endowed with conscious life and with the capacity to "make" or "break" our lives by deciding for the possibilities that present themselves to us.

Man is born for life; this is revealed not only in the Bible but in man's very nature itself. By this we mean not just that man has a spiritual principle which is "incorruptible" and "immortal"—his soul—but that the whole man, as a being capable of decision, of love, and of self-surrender, is oriented toward a perfection of life that is to be achieved only in total self-giving in response to a totality of love beyond all human experience or comprehension.

Yet this unlimited natural possibility is, to our anguish, discovered in actual experience to be so limited, so restricted, so frustrated, and so ambiguous as to produce not hope but only despair. Indeed, the ambiguities of our human hope are sometimes so acute as to reduce life itself, one might think, to a complete absurdity. But now, in the Nativity of Christ, the Great Joy is announced, in which all the ambiguities are swept aside and all men are confronted with the clear possibility of a decision that will not only help them to put together the pieces of lives wrecked in individual failure but will even make sense out of the lives of all men of all time.

Take courage, for I have come to announce to you the Great Joy, the joy of all the people, for today there is born to you in the city of David a Savior who is Christ, the Anointed One, the Lord [LUKE 2:10–11].

The Nativity Gospel is, then, the announcement of life. He who has come into the world has come "in order that they might have life" in all fullness and abundance, life without limitation and without restraint (John 10:10). St. Irenaeus, one of the earliest of the Fathers, built his anthropology on the fact that God became a child. Christ came into the world to recapitulate the whole work of creation and all of man's history since Adam. Irenaeus did not invent this idea—he took it from St. Paul (Ephesians 1:10).

When a knot is to be untied, the string must be drawn back by the way it first traveled when the knot was tied. Christ came to fulfill God's original plan for man, and he started over again from the beginning, as the second Adam, to do the work that Adam had bungled, to untie the hard knot that Adam had tied in sin. In Christ we therefore see man as he is intended to be: a child of God, capable of growth in God, a child for whom growth as man is growth to find himself in God, for whom maturity is the fullness of the stature and the likeness of God in Christ (Ephesians 3:14–20; 4:9–16). In the mere recital of the Nativity there is, for the Christian attuned to the whole of Biblical revelation, a realization that life is a knot which, in Christ, has been completely untied. The Christian call to freedom is a call to be, as Christ himself, an untied knot.

It is in this sense that the message of Christmas is eschatological: it is the revelation and celebration of the new age in which we live, in which our humanity has been restored to us untrammeled and disentangled, in Christ. The sense of new birth and of childhood which is communicated by the perfect literary artistry of Luke conveys to us this truth. In hearing the account of the Nativity in Luke, we are stirred not only by the literary quality of the words but even more by the theological undertones of this profound message which is in fact completely revolutionary and which the Church alone can fully understand: we are created anew in the incarnation of the Word. Our humanity has been seized and taken up by the person of the Word. Humanity can never be the same after this fact. The possibilities of life and fulfillment which had been closed in Adam, and to which no religious philosophy, no mystery cult, no mystic wisdom could reopen the way, can become ours again *simply because we are men,* now that Christ has become man.

Yet the Church's understanding of this truth is quite different from that of any religious mystique or spiritual philosophy. It is not that man's nature is restored to life, but that *each human person* has the option of accepting or rejecting the new life which Christ offers us because we are men. Because we share the *human nature* which he took in the Incarnation, we are capable of this new life. But it is *by our decision as persons,* that is, by our belief, our acceptance of life *in the person of Christ,* our response as persons to his personal and saving love, that our manhood is seized and transformed by the life-giving Spirit. Thus, Christ is born in our nature that we may be reborn in the fullest sense as persons.

The full Christian sense of the person is found in the recovery of our likeness of God, in Christ, by his Spirit. This, in turn, is attained only in that relationship of personal love that is established, in the Church, with all who have heard the same message and responded to it in the one Spirit. It is this grace, this stupendous gift and possibility, this power to be made new, not only individually, but as *Ecclesia,* as *"one new man,"* which is announced in the great joy of the Nativity Gospel. It is the theological fact which the Church celebrates in the paschal liturgy and which is extended to all feasts, especially to Christmas, with proper individual aspects.

The details of the Nativity—the way it is related, the incidents that are selected by each evangelist, the theological points that each one emphasizes—all serve to bring home to us this inner revelation, which the Church at once announces (in her kerygma) and celebrates (in her liturgy). Matthew, for instance, seeks to show in how many ways the birth of Christ is the fulfillment of the Old Testament messianic prophecies, and therefore how, in Christ, the whole meaning and aspiration of the Old Testament is completed and made plain. Luke, with a human and compassionate charm, brings out what St. Paul called the goodness of God and his tender love for men (Titus 3:4). Whether or not Luke sat down and dutifully took it all down at the dictation of the Blessed Mother we can hardly know; but the fact remains that there is a feminine aspect in the Nativity recital according to Luke. This tenderness (so well expressed in the *umilenye* icons of the Russian Church) fills out the theological picture of God's mercy to man in the Incarnation. Tender maternal love is inseparable from the whole theology of Mary the Mother of God.

We may argue until doomsday about whether the angel who appeared to Mary came in through the window or through the wall, whether it was midnight or ten in the morning, or, indeed, whether there was an angel at all (was it perhaps just a bright idea?). The fact remains that in this narrative of the miraculous virgin birth of the Lord, as recited in the early Church, we have a revelation of the infinite motherly compassion of God for men, a revelation which is not only absolutely without error but which, by reason of the special "feminine" cast of its literary expression, tells us something quite unique that we would otherwise never apprehend. (Modern psychology makes us aware, for example, of the severe limitations of a theology built exclusively on an authoritarian father-image, and the importance of a concept of sonship in which the mysteries of the Mother and of the Holy Spirit are needed to fill out the full meaning of the redemptive love of the Savior on the Cross. The Nativity Gospels provide something of this essential theological element in our soteriology.)

Now it is this unique aspect of the divine mercy, an aspect which is so powerfully suggested by the poetry of Luke but can never be reduced to scientific language, that is precisely what the Christian heart obscurely senses in responding to the Gospel of the Nativity as read and understood by the Church.

In the *living situation* created now by liturgical celebration, now by the Gospels, God makes clear to the faithful member of Christ the meaning and the reality of the life which he does, in fact, receive in his heart from Christ at the very moment when he reads or hears the message of joy. It is this precise spiritual reality and experience which the medieval writers were trying to bring out in their often oblique and illogical ways of explaining the sense of the Scriptures. Medieval exegesis, from the scientific point of view, seldom rises above the level of arbitrary and childish nonsense. But as a religious fact, as an expression of the living experience of Christ in the Church, it is sometimes a witness that cannot be disputed, even though it may have taken a form that no longer makes it accessible to most men of our time.

Needless to say, this constitutes no sweeping defense of a habit of allegorizing in which everything signified something else and, as a result, nothing seemed to signify anything definite. But let us remember that if a St. Bernard, for example, interprets the water pots at the marriage of Cana to mean various monastic observances which Christ will turn "into wine," he is stating a definite theological truth about the life in which "good works" receive their significance, not from juridical exactitude and official approbation, but from the transforming action of the Holy Spirit. This flows from an authentic Christian reading of the liturgical texts of the Christmas season as the message of "new life" and "new creation" in the Incarnation.

This, then, is our main point: the Nativity Gospels tell us first of all that new life is given us in Christ the Lord, the incarnate Word (see especially John 1). While announcing this to us, the Gospel message also enables us, by the way in which it is expressed, to experience something of the mysterious reality which is announced, and which can never be reduced to precise and objective terminology. This awareness becomes accessible to us, not by virtue of special gifts or technical training (though these things may have very great value in expanding the range of our apprehension), but above all by faith. Faith that responds to the possibility of salvation and fulfillment opened to us in the person of Jesus Christ matures, by the very fact of its sincere response, into a personal understanding of the implications of this commitment, a personal realization of what it means to belong entirely to Christ.

However, we must not overemphasize the element of experience, since the revelation of Christ in the Gospels is not a matter of religious psychology but of living theology. But we must not separate theology from the prayer of the Church. Theology is not merely the understanding which the expert has but the revelation which the Church has. This revelation, which remains as fresh and new today as it was in the days of St. Irenaeus or the apostles, remains accessible to every Christian who enters into the living experience of Christ in the Church. Hence the monastic dictum: "The true theologian is the man of prayer." It is by the Bible above all, the Bible read in the sacred assembly or meditated in the intimacy of silent prayer, that this knowledge of Christ is laid open to us.

The Church's experience of the revelation of Christ is not a static illumination—it is a dynamic mode of life. Too long have we assumed that it was enough to make up our minds and give intellectual assent to authoritatively declared truths, and that this was the whole of faith. Christian faith is not just a habit by which we are inclined to give assent to certain dogmatic information; it is a conversion of our whole being, a surrender of the entire person to Christ in His Church. It is an act of penance, the most fundamental act of penance, the metanoia of entire change of heart which leads to the abandonment of our old understanding of ourselves, of our relation to God and to the world, and to the discovery of our new identity in Christ.

The announcement of the birth of Christ is, therefore, not only a revelation of joy, but an intimation of anguish and conflict. He has come into the world as a sign of contradiction (again it is Luke who speaks—3:34), and even the heart of His Mother must be pierced with a sword of sorrow. In the Gospel of compassion and life we encounter also the Gospel of passion, of anguish, of death. Mark, who does not give us a Nativity recital, devotes his whole Gospel to Christ as the sign that is contradicted. But it is in death and contradiction that death is overcome by life and contradiction by transcendent truth.

If we, believing that God has spoken to us entirely and definitively in Christ (Hebrews 1:1–2), accept God's revelation of Himself in the Infant of Bethlehem, we must realize also that this acceptance has grave consequences for our lives. It means accepting One for whom there is no room in the "inn" of an excited and distraught world which is also, without knowing it, entering a new eschatological dimension. We see this in the disturbing symbol of that census which brings "the whole world" into the books of a Roman imperial power. If we accept this Infant as our God, then we accept our own obligation to grow with Him in a world of arrogant power and travel with Him as He ascends to Jerusalem and to the Cross, which is the denial of power.

It is not enough to respond to the joy and charm of Bethlehem. We must recognize that if we belong to Christ, we must die with Him in order to rise with Him. That is to say that our decision to accept God's revelation of Himself in Christ implied, by that very fact, a decision to accept His revelation of *ourselves* in Christ. Christ is God and Man. He is the revelation of God in man. He is also the revelation of man in God. If I accept the revelation of God in Christ, I must also accept the revelation of man in Christ, realizing that, from the point of view of the Gospels, without the Cross and without the Resurrection, *there can be no full meaning in the life of man.* If the Cross is God's "No" to worldly arrogance, then our decision for Christ must be a renunciation of all reliance on worldly power.

The decision to accept Christ as the revelation of God's plan for the world is, then, an inexorable renunciation of any attempt to live on two levels at once: one a sacred level, the level of the soul, of "spirituality," of "recollection" and of goodness; and the other a material level of work, distraction, legitimate recreation, power politics, and so on, all of it real enough but somehow unrelated to what goes on in church or in my "interior castle." If Christ is the revelation of the whole meaning of man, if this meaning of man's life is solely and entirely to be found in the fact that *man is a child of God,* then everything in my life becomes relevant or irrelevant in proportion as it tends to my growth as a member of Christ, as a child of God, and to the extension of Christ in the world of man through his Church.

Hence, the Nativity Gospel remains a Gospel of renewal, and we can, without stretching the idea at all far, call it a Gospel of *aggiornamento.* The new life which the Church seeks today is precisely this: the Christ-life, the life of "the spirit," not in the sense of "more spirituality," but in the sense of being possessed and anointed by *the* Spirit, the Spirit of Christ, the Holy Spirit.

Here again, in the Gospel of Luke especially, we encounter the presence of the Holy Spirit overshadowing the Virgin Mother in the new creation as He had overshadowed the abyss of unformed matter in the first creation. Though the Spirit was to be given to the Church only at the Resurrection and at the Pentecost, He is already present in the Church's recital of the Nativity. Our acceptance of God's gift of Himself to us in Christ means, ultimately, our acceptance of the Holy Spirit by whom Christ is born in us, lives in us, grows in us, suffers, dies, and rises in us.

It is because we have received His Spirit in baptism and in the sacraments that we are able to recognize Christ when the word of his Nativity is proclaimed in the liturgy of the Church. It is the life of the Holy Spirit in us that moves us to respond "Amen" to the Church's prayer to the Father, in Christ. It is the Spirit Himself who, having made us other Christs, cries out to the Father in us (Romans 8:14–16) in that "free" and confident speech of sons (*parrhesia*) liberated from the Law of fear. For the Spirit teaches us that if we are born with Christ, and die with Christ, we are co-heirs with Him in the Great Joy which is His victory over death, and in His meekness, which has inherited the earth.